D1192196

THE SLUMP IN EUROPE

THE SLUMP IN EUROPE

Reconstructing Open Economy Theory

Jean-Paul Fitoussi
and
Edmund S. Phelps

Basil Blackwell

First published 1988

Basil Blackwell Ltd
108 Cowley Road, Oxford, OX4 1JF, UK

Basil Blackwell Inc,
432 Park Avenue South, Suite 1503
New York, NY 10016, USA

British Library Cataloguing in Publication Data

Fitoussi, Jean-Paul
The slump in Europe: reconstructing
open economy theory.
1. Europe – Economic conditions –
1945-
I. Title   II. Phelps, Edmund S.
330.94′0558   HC240
ISBN 0-631-15557-0

Library of Congress Cataloging in Publication Data

Fitoussi, Jean-Paul
The slump in Europe

Bibliography: p.
Includes index.
1. Unemployment – Europe. 2. Europe – Economic
conditions – 1945– .
I. Phelps, Edmund S. II. Title.
HD5764.A6F58 1988   330.94′0558   87–25693
ISBN 0–631–15557–0

Typeset in Times 12/14pt
by Columns of Reading
Printed in Great Britain by
Billings & Son Ltd, Worcester

Contents

Preface   vii

1 The Problem for Analysis   1
1.1 Magnitude of the Slump   1
1.2 Existing Explanations   2
1.3 New Directions   8
1.4 Plan of the Book   10

2 Stylized Facts   13
2.1 Exchange Rate Movements   14
2.2 Real Interest Rates   17
2.3 User Cost of Capital   19
2.4 Wage Shares   21
2.5 Mark-ups   23
2.6 Average Product of Labor   27
2.7 Investment   28
2.8 Relative Price of Capital Goods   32
2.9 (Un)employment   33

3. Orthodox Theory   35
3.1 The Standard Propositions and
Qualifications   36
3.2 The Essential Orthodox Model   40

4. Elements of a Reconstructed Theory   53

4.1 Customer Markets in the Transmission of Foreign Shocks 56

4.2 Capital Mechanisms in the Transmission of Real Interest Shocks 66

4.3 Real Investment-good Prices in the Transmission of Shocks 78

4.4 The Persistence of the Slump in Europe: Our Supply-price View 89

5 An Examination of Demand-side Explanations 97

5.1 The Fiscal Austerity Hypothesis 97

5.2 The Tight Money Hypothesis 112

5.3 The Hysteresis Effect Required by Demand-side Explanations 117

6 Can Europe Do It? 125

Selected References 133

Index 137

Preface

In reviewing the current explanations of the 1980s slump in Europe, we found that they could not account for the most striking features of the period. Each country's experience, moreover, needed a special theory. The synchronism of the evolution of unemployment in different countries was a coincidence according to this kind of theorizing.

With this book we present a new explanation of the slump in Europe built upon the central features of the 1980s – the record heights reached by real interest rates and the extraordinary appreciation, eventually reversed, of the US dollar. The first feature is ignored, and the second misinterpreted, we argue, by existing theory. Ours is a unified explanation of possible application outside Europe, as well as inside.

Estimates that real interest rates have now moderated and the dollar returned to earth seemingly compel us to predict that a recovery in Europe is now under way. We observe that in fact unemployment did improve significantly in Britain and Germany from 1985 to 1986 and output and employment accelerated in Italy over the same period; however it is also true

[vii]

that the recovery has been slow and far from universal and this recovery has faltered in 1987. We also observe that the moderation of expected real interest rates is slight and at risk, and we note that the yen has climbed as the dollar has descended.

It remains urgent to address, as we do, the question of what Europe can and should do to ensure and hasten the recovery of employment from the unacceptable levels at which it stands.

The research on which this book is based was undertaken for the Commission of the European Communities, Directorate General Employment, Social Affairs and Education, and we are most grateful to them, particularly to John Morley, for their support.

1

The Problem for Analysis

1.1 Magnitude of the Slump

Our subject is the alarming rise of unemployment in Europe during the 1980s. We speak of the slump in Europe rather than a "European slump" since this slump, we argue, is tied to external forces, many of which are contractionary elsewhere as well as in Europe.

Whatever the criterion used to judge the performance of the European economies, one must conclude that this depression has no historical precedent outside the 1930s. The rate of growth of the gross domestic product in the period 1981–85 averaged less than 1 percent as compared to 2.4 percent in the 1974–79 period and 4.6 percent in the preceding 5 years.

More striking, the average rate of growth of the European countries, which had evolved *pari passu* with that of the rest of the OECD from 1960 to 1979, has in the period 1981–85 fallen to less than half of the growth rate of the OECD countries combined (0.9 percent as compared to 2 percent); see table 1.1.

No wonder then that the rate of unemployment has

been continuously rising in Europe, in spite of the numerous measures devised to reduce the labor supply – reduction in working time, early retirements and so on; see table 1.2.

1.2 Existing Explanations

A popular explanation, especially in America, one appealing to Keynesian economics, points to the fiscal austerity in Europe: the shrinkage of public services and public sector capital expenditures, and the maintenance of tax rates at pre-slump highs. The European austerity is often contrasted with the activist budgetary deficits run elsewhere; the red ink in the United States and, earlier, Japan, particularly.

But this hypothesis forgets some offsetting mechanisms: if increased public spending "crowds out", however much or little, then decreased public spending crowds in – not in the first month or year, perhaps, but presumably within 5 years. What is the effect on aggregate employment? In Keynesian theory reduced public expenditure or increased tax rates by a monetarist Europe – whether in an open economy with a freely fluctuating exchange rate or in a hypothetical closed economy – reduces total domestic expenditure and hence employment only in so far as it lowers the rate of interest, which slows the velocity of money. However, there is no evidence of either. Interest rates and velocity have been high in recent years. The same theory also says that the nations with the greatest fiscal austerity will suffer the most.

[2]

TABLE 1.1 Growth rates of GDP, 1961–86

	1961–67[a]	1968–73[a]	1974–79[a]	1980–84[a]	1974	1975	1976	1977	1978	1979	1980	1981	1982	1983	1984	1985	1986
USA	4.5	3.5	2.6	2.0	−0.9	−0.8	4.7	5.5	4.7	2.6	−0.4	3.4	−3.0	2.9	7.2	2.5	2.5
Japan	10.5	9.5	3.7	4.2	−1.2	2.6	4.8	5.3	5.1	5.2	4.4	3.9	2.8	3.1	5.8	4.6	3.2
Germany (FRG)	4.8	5.1	2.5	0.9	0.3	−1.6	5.4	3.0	2.9	4.2	1.4	0.2	−0.6	1.2	2.6	2.5	3.5
France	5.7	5.6	3.1	1.2	3.2	0.2	5.2	3.1	3.8	3.3	1.1	0.5	1.8	0.7	1.3	1.3	2.3
UK	3.2	3.4	1.5	0.7	−1.0	−0.7	3.8	1.0	3.6	2.2	−2.3	−1.4	1.5	3.4	1.8	3.3	2.6
Italy	5.7	4.9	2.6	1.0	4.1	−3.6	5.9	1.9	2.7	4.9	3.9	0.2	−0.5	−0.4	2.6	2.3	2.7
EEC (12)	4.8	4.9	2.5	0.9	2.0	−1.0	4.9	2.4	3.1	3.2	1.2	−0.1	0.6	1.2	2.0	2.3	2.7
OECD	5.1	4.6	2.6	1.9	0.6	−0.3	4.7	3.5	4.1	3.0	1.2	1.6	−0.6	2.6	4.7	3.0	

Sources: *European Economy*, various issues and OECD *Economic Outlook*, December 1986 for the average rate of the OECD countries.
[a] Yearly average rate.

TABLE 1.2 Unemployment rates

	1960–67	1968–73	1974–79	1973	1974	1975	1976	1977	1978	1979	1980	1981	1982	1983	1984	1985	1986
USA	5.1	4.7	6.8	4.9	5.6	8.5	7.7	7.1	6.0	5.8	7.1	7.6	9.7	9.6	7.5	7.2	6.9
Japan	1.4	1.2	1.9	1.3	1.4	1.9	2.0	2.0	2.2	2.1	2.0	2.2	2.4	2.7	2.7	2.6	2.9
Germany	0.8	0.9	3.6	1.1	2.3	4.1	4.0	4.0	3.8	3.3	3.4	4.8	6.9	8.4	8.4	8.5	7.8
France	0.7	1.5	4.4	1.8	2.3	3.9	4.2	4.8	5.2	5.9	6.4	7.7	8.7	8.8	9.9	10.3	10.6
UK	1.7	2.6	4.3	2.2	2.2	3.6	4.9	5.3	5.1	4.7	6.0	9.2	10.6	11.6	11.8	12.1	12.0
Italy	5.7	4.8	5.7	4.9	4.9	5.3	5.6	5.4	6.1	6.7	7.2	8.0	9.7	10.9	11.9	12.8	12.7
EEC (9)	2.1	2.3	4.6	2.4	2.9	4.3	4.8	5.0	5.2	5.2	5.8	7.7	9.3	10.4	10.9	11.1	10.8

Source: *European Economy* no. 29, July 1986. Yearly average as percentage of the civilian labor force, 1960–86.

[3]

However Italy, which least illustrates fiscal austerity, has not been spared the slump.[1]

The favored explanation in Europe itself is what we might call the Pigouvian explanation. It is really a class of solutions all resting on the hypothesis of what has come to be called real wage rigidity. Its strength comes from its integration in a general equilibrium model within the non-Walrasian tradition.[2] In particular, works on general equilibrium with rationing have emphasized the theoretical possibility of classical unemployment.[3] In such a framework – given the configuration of policy variables – a too high level of the (exogenously given) real wage could be at the origin of unemployment. This conclusion remains true even when prices are flexible and the product market clears. The source of the trouble is then associated with the existence of price linkages and especially wage indexation.[4] Indeed the assumption of real wage rigidity, though it can be traced back to Pigou, undoubtedly draws some of its current inspiration from the early formulations of implicit or explicit employment contracts in which no motive arises for anything less than full indexation of the contractual nominal wage to the consumer price index. Since European labor markets are characterized by immobility, which makes long-term contracts desired, and since the European labor force is heavily unionized, which means that the institutional apparatus for the implementation and enforcement of contracts is at hand, Europe is fertile ground for the hypothesis that the money wage rates of existing employees will insistently keep pace with the consumer price level, even when

[4]

supply shocks or other real shocks render the real wage invariance inconsistent with employees' continuation at work with full pay. In this view, only new entrants can lever the average real wage upward or downward.

Economists who have examined and endorsed this hypothesis compare the real wage (conceptually, the wage in terms of consumables) with the high-employment wage as proxied by an estimate of the marginal productivity of labor (also expressed in consumables). If the real wage somehow rises – "rigidity" here is an ill-chosen term for resistance, since an optimal response of the real wage to the change in some elasticity or even sheer animal spirits is not really precluded – or the marginal productivity falls, this widening of the "real wage gap," the percentage excess of real wage over marginal product, is said to cause a fall of employment.[5]

This approach seems too unreliable, in fact, to warrant treating the evidence it collects as decisive. Indeed, it could lead us to confuse covariations with causality. An increase in the gap is neither necessary nor sufficient evidence of supply-side effects acting to contract employment. Evidence, if such existed, that everyone's real wage had increased while unemployment rose would not demonstrate that the former caused the latter. An employment-contracting demand disturbance may push up the average real wage in the process, because prices are faster to respond than are wages, as Keynes supposed in his *General Theory*, or because the workers laid off are disproportionately from among the low-paid, but that is not sufficient

[5]

evidence of the rise in anyone's real asking price at high (full) employment or a fall of anyone's marginal product at full employment.[6] So the increase of the real wage gap is not sufficient to show that a supply shock has occurred. On the other hand the gap methodology supposes that employment declines that are in fact initiated by supply-type shocks will be evidenced by unusually large rises in the real wage gap, but not all such shocks raise the real wage gap. An upward disturbance to price mark-ups, for example, will presumably contract employment; but such a rise of mark-ups will reduce or leave unchanged the real wage gap because it will presumably reduce or leave unchanged the real wage, depending on the degree of indexation, and leave unaffected labor's marginal product. So a rise of the real wage is not a necessary consequence of the supply shock.

More generally, empirical research designed to assert the classical nature of present-day unemployment has too often been cast in a partial equilibrium framework,[7] and such has particularly been the case in studies on the "real wage gap" and NAIRU, the non-accelerating inflation rate of unemployment.

Recognizing that real wages are not volatile, and thus not likely to be a "prime mover" of the system, many economists see the cause of the recent slump in the second oil-price shock, in 1979, juxtaposed against European real-wage rigidity. But the course of events has been so different after the second oil shock than after the first that it seems to us difficult to appeal to the same factors to explain both episodes.

The classical nature of unemployment in Europe in

the mid-1970s has been a widely accepted hypothesis. The stagflation of that period lends credence to that thesis. However, the 1980s, which combines steadily rising unemployment and rapid disinflation, should at least be examined with a fresh analysis. If we compare Europe and the USA in these two periods, we see that between 1973 and 1979 the business cycle seems to be rather synchronized between the two regions. This is clearly not the case after the second oil shock, and for the first time since the Second World War the unemployment rate has become higher in Europe than in the USA. Although on average in the years 1983 to 1985 the annual rate of growth of output in the USA is about what it was in the pre-first-oil-shock period, it is almost three times lower in Europe. Something else is thus needed to explain this lasting period of slump in Europe, and the divergences between the two regions.

The preceding explanations appear thus to be incomplete, and we propose in this book to take another route towards a reconstruction of open economy theory. That does not mean that imperfect flexibility of real wages or demand deficiency will be no part of any of the stories to be told, but that we will frame our explanation in terms of a two-country general equilibrium model where other relative prices – real rate of interest, real exchange rate, real price of capital goods – will play an essential role as well. We do not want just to blame the lack of "profitable" productive capacity for the rise of European unemployment. We want also to understand why capacity has not been sufficiently profitable to operate and to expand.[8] We shall show that other factors than

[7]

the real wage have provided the driving forces in the 1980s.

As we believe that much of the difference between the slump of the 1970s and the (much worse) slump of the 1980s can be assigned to the change in the policy regime in the USA – a change in both its monetary and fiscal policy – our model will portray a two-region world economy consisting of "America" and "Europe".

1.3   New Directions

A first line of argument to explain the slump could rely on induced policy reactions in Europe aimed at counterbalancing the real appreciation of the dollar initiated in 1981. American policies have had an *indirect* role in the European slump through their influence on European demand management.

Imported inflation became a sufficiently serious problem to lead the FRG, among others, to adopt a vigorously restrictive monetary policy. In view of its weight in Europe, FRG monetary policy set the tone for the other European countries.[9] The apparatus of the European Monetary System operated to hinder the inclinations of the more permissive countries to devalue against the Mark and, accordingly, to allow an increase in the supply of money. It could be further argued that as greater slack in the economy combined with higher interest rates to yield increased budget deficits, fiscal policy became more restrictive as a result.[10] Although a substantial part of the cutback in public expenditure may have "crowded in" an off-setting amount of exports, it could also be that this fiscal policy has not been without "effectiveness", curtailing aggregate demand and, as a side-effect, constricting output and employment.

We have no wish to deny European monetary and fiscal policies any part in the rise of European unemployment. In fact, a contribution of our modeling is a persuasive reason why public spending is not completely offset by crowding out of net exports. In addition, the claim that European demand management showed a contractionary response to the disturbances from overseas fits in well enough with our theme of US influence on European employment. But whether these policy reactions play a decisive or essential, part in the slump is another question. To answer this question we need to know what would have been the course of employment and growth in Europe if the instruments of European demand management had not changed. Is it possible that the fiscal and monetary shocks originating in the USA in the early 1980s provide a sufficient explanation of the European slump, leaving aside the other factors? In tackling the problem this way we know that the risk is to overemphasize the role of supply factors – particularly direct external factors – in the analysis. But this role seems to have been neglected in the study of the subject and we do not have to lose sight of domestic demand factors when focusing at first on the direct mechanisms – external supply and external demand.

In a nutshell, our explanation will assign a crucial role to the package of policy innovations in the USA and will introduce some new theoretical elements to understand the mechanisms through which these shocks have been transmitted to Europe. Our explanation is in the category of general equilibrium theory with linked prices[11] as our models portray prices to be linked to foreign exchange through the markup in foreign markets, and wages to be linked to prices by law or contractual agreements. We will also emphasize, as part of the same general framework, the cost or supply effects of real interest rates.

1.4 Plan of the Book

The plan of the book is as follows. In chapter 2 we turn to the facts, stylized or not, with which our models ought to be consistent. With chapter 3 we take up the international transmission of foreign shocks, beginning with a review of the implications of orthodox open-economy theory. Chapters 4 and 5 will be devoted to the development of our theory. The first of these chapters takes up certain mechanisms operating from the cost or price side, and the second of these chapters returns to the demand side from the perspective of our reconstructed open-economy theory. Chapter 6 will consider some remedies for the European slump that are pointed to by our theory.

Notes

1   We will come back to the question of the responsibility borne by Europe's own policies in chapter 5.
2   For a survey of this line of thinking, cf. J.-P. Fitoussi, "Modern macroeconomic theory: an overview," in J.-P. Fitoussi (ed.), *Modern Macroeconomic Theory* (Oxford: Basil Blackwell, 1983).
3   See in particular E. Malinvaud: *The Theory of Unemployment Reconsidered* (Oxford: Basil Blackwell, 1977).
4   For an overview on "supply constrained equilibria," cf. J.-H. Drèze, "Underemployment equilibria," *European Economic Review*, 31(1/2), February/March 1987. A macroeconomic application of this concept is in P. Dehez and J.-P. Fitoussi: "Wage indexation and macroeconomic fluctuations," in W. Beckerman (ed.), *Unemployment and Wage Rigidity* (Baltimore: Johns Hopkins Press, 1986).
5   The basic methods are in M. Bruno and J. D. Sachs, *Economics of Worldwide Stagflation*, Harvard University Press, 1985. See also M. Bruno, "Aggregate supply and demand factors in OECD unemployment: an update" *Economica*, vol. 53 (supplement 1986). J. D. Sachs, "High unemployment in Europe," Working Paper no. 1830, National Bureau of Economic Research, February 1986.
6   For a comprehensive study, see J.-P. Fitoussi and others, *Real Wages and Unemployment*, Report to the European Economic Community (Brussels, December 1985, mimeo).
7   There exist notable exceptions; cf. e.g. P. Artus, G. Laroque and G. Michel, "Estimation of a quarterly macro-economic model with quantity rationing," *Econometrica*, 52, 1387–1414, 1984; H. Sneessens and J. H. Drèze, "A discussion of Belgian unemployment, combining traditional concepts and disequilibrium econometrics," *Economica* 53, S89–S119.
8   On this point an explanation which is consistent with ours, yet distinct from it, can be found in E. Malinvaud, "The legacy of European stagflation," *European Economic*

Review, 31(1/2), February/March 1987.

9 Different kinds of policies were tried in some countries, e.g. France in 1981–82, but they had sooner or later to be withdrawn so as to follow the common line.

10 See M. Feldstein, "US budget deficits and the European economies: resolving the political puzzle," *American Economic Review*, May 1986.

11 See M. Kurz, "Unemployment equilibrium in an economy with linked prices," *Journal of Economic Theory*, February 1982 for the micro-foundations of this approach, and P. Dehez and J.-P. Fitoussi, "Equilibres de stagflation et indexation des salaires," in J.-P. -Fitoussi and P.-A. Muet (eds), *Macrodynamique et déséquilibres*, Economica, 1987, for a macroeconomic application of this framework.

2

Stylized Facts

There are no facts, only interpretations
(Nietzsche).

In view of the differences in the periods following the two oil shocks, something else is needed to explain the 1980s slump than the sheer increase in the price of oil. Accordingly we want to focus our attention on those facts which give distinctiveness to the 1980s.

When one is able to look from some historical distance at the 1980s, one will no doubt be struck by two specific features of the period: the huge fluctuations of the nominal exchange rates of the European countries *vis-à-vis* the dollar; and the worldwide increase in the rate of interest, nominal and real, to historical highs. It would be very strange indeed if these undisputed facts had not a significant influence on the economic performances of the countries concerned.

2.1 Exchange rate movements

The real exchange rate of all European currencies in terms of the US-dollar fell by more than 40 percent between the third quarter of 1980 and the first quarter of 1985. The extent of the depreciation does not seem to depend on the way the real exchange rate is measured; whether the nominal exchange rate is adjusted for differential movements in unit labor cost, or whether it is adjusted for differential movements in consumer price indices, the figures are about the same. On average the depreciation was larger during the first half of the period than during the second.

This has to be contrasted with the 1970s, where the dollar was depreciating in real terms *vis-à-vis* all European currencies, and where the two measures of the depreciation were significantly different. The figures are shown in table 2.1. The first column gives for each country the rate of change of the nominal exchange rate adjusted for differential movements in unit labor costs (sl^*):

$$\dot{sl}^* = \dot{e}^* + \dot{ulc} - \dot{ulc}^*$$

The second column gives the rate of change of the nominal exchange rate, adjusted for differential movements in consumer price indices (sp^*)

$$\dot{sp}^* = \dot{e} + \dot{p} - \dot{p}^*$$

[14]

TABLE 2.1 Real appreciation and depreciation of European currencies *vis-à-vis* the dollar (1970–86) (percentages)

Periods	FRG			France			Italy			UK		
	$\dot{s}l^{*a}$	$\dot{s}p^{*b}$	$\dot{s}l^* - \dot{s}p^*$	$\dot{s}l^{*a}$	$\dot{s}p^{*b}$	$\dot{s}l^* - \dot{s}p^*$	$\dot{s}l^{*a}$	$\dot{s}p^{*b}$	$\dot{s}l^* - \dot{s}p^*$	$\dot{s}l^{*a}$	$\dot{s}p^{*b}$	$\dot{s}l^* - \dot{s}p^*$
1970–1973.3	77.4	57.3	20.1	56	39.1	16.9	42.4	17.8	24.6	29.1	15.2	13.9
1973.3–1980.3	7.6	0.6	7	17.9	14.6	3.3	13.6	10	3.6	78.6	47.9	30.7
1970–1980.3	90.8	58.3	32.5	84	59.4	24.6	61.7	28.4	33.3	130.6	70.4	60.2
1980.3–1982.3	−30.5	−31.6	1.1	−34.5	−36.2	1.7	−28.6	−29.3	0.7	−29	−25.8	−3.2
1982.3–1985.1	−23.2	−24.8	1.6	−19.5	−22.1	2.6	−15.2	−15.6	0.4	−31	−33.1	2.1
1980.3–1985.1	−46.6	−48.6	2	−47.2	−50.3	3.1	−39.5	−40.3	0.8	−51.1	−50.3	−0.8
1985.1–1986.4	72.5	55	17.5	54.1	53.5	0.6	64	54.2	9.8	38.2	32.7	5.5

[a] $\dot{s}l^*$ = Rate of change of the nominal exchange rate against the dollar adjusted for differential movements in unit labor costs.
[b] $\dot{s}p^*$ = Rate of change of the nominal exchange rate against the dollar adjusted for differential movements in consumer price indices.

Source: authors' calculations using data from the Bureau of Labor Statistics and from OECD. The new revised series on unit labor cost have been used.

[15]

where: $\dot{e}^*$ is the rate of change of the nominal exchange rate defined here as the number of dollars per unit of the various European currencies;

$\dot{ulc}^*$ is the rate of change of unit labor cost in the USA;

$\dot{p}^*$ is the rate of change of the consumer price index in the USA;

$\dot{ulc}$ and p are defined correspondingly for each of the four European countries considered.

The difference between $\dot{sl}^*$ and $\dot{sp}^*$, the third column of table 2.1 for each country, is thus equal to:

$$\dot{sl}^* - \dot{sp}^* = (\dot{p}^* - \dot{ulc}^*) - (\dot{p} - \dot{ulc}).$$

which is the difference between the rates of change of the mark-up of consumer prices over unit labor cost in the USA and in the various European countries. A positive difference means that the mark-up is increasing more (decreasing less) in the USA than in the other countries, and conversely.

It thus appears that during the entire period depicted in table 2.1 the mark-up in the USA deterioriated less or widened more than in the other countries. But it also appears that, when the dollar is depreciating, the increase in the relative markup of US firms is rather pronounced, as can be seen in the 1970s or in the more recent period beginning in the first quarter of 1985. Hence, beyond the sheer noticing of the real appreciation of the dollar and of its extent,

[16]

a derived stylized fact is also established:

In the first half of the 1980s, when the European currencies were depreciating against the dollar, the tendency of the relative mark-up of the European firms to decrease in relation to US firms was interrupted.

, In section 2.5 we shall present our evidence on the absolute, as distinct from the comparative, behavior of the mark-up in Europe relative to trend.

2.2 Real Interest Rates

Real rates of interest have been at historic highs from 1982 onwards. This is generally agreed upon, even if there is no satisfactory way of measuring the real interest rate and thus of charting its course. But whichever way is chosen, this assessment is barely affected.

During the period 1981–85 the conventionally measured long-term interest rate[1] has averaged between 4 and 5 percent in the countries of the EEC and more than 6 percent in the USA. Short-term real rates of interest have been lower in Europe than in the USA, by about two percentage points, though much higher than in the 1970s. The fact that these rates were about zero or negative in the 1970s – an exception being the FRG – should be underlined.

The conventional measure (rows (a) in table 2.2) probably underestimates the level of real interest rates. If we take into account the expected decelera-

TABLE 2.2 **Real long-term interest rates***

	1979	1980	1981	1982	1983	1984	1985	1986
France								
(a)	−1.3	−0.3	2.4	3.9	4	5.1	5.1	6.3
(b)	−2.4	−0.3	3.2	5.1	5.2	5.9	7.3	6.2
FRG								
(a)	3.3	3.1	4.1	3.6	4.6	5.4	4.7	6.2
(b)	2.7	2.7	4.6	4.7	5.1	5.3	5.5	5.7
Italy								
(a)	−0.7	−5.1	1.9	4.6	3.4	4.1	3.8	4.5
(b)	−3.6	−3.8	3.1	5.5	5.4	4.9	5.6	5.1
UK								
(a)	−0.4	−4.2	2.8	4.3	6.2	5.7	4.5	6.3
(b)	−2.5	−0.8	4.6	6.6	6	5.2	6.1	6.1
USA								
(a)	−1.9	−2	3.5	6.9	7.9	8.1	7	5.8
(b)	−2.9	−0.3	5.9	8.6	7.4	8.5	8	5.2

* Nominal long-term rates are defined as follows: average yield to maturity of central government bonds with terms of 10 years for the USA. Average yield to maturity of National Equipment Bonds of 1965, 1966, and 1967 for France, public authorities bonds with terms of 3 years or more for the FRG, bonds issued by the Consortium of Credit for Public Works with an average maturity of 15 to 20 years for Italy, and central government bonds with 20 years to maturity for the UK.
Source: IMF, *World Economic Outlook*, April 1987, table A.15.
(a) Real rates are calculated by subtracting from the nominal rate the current rate of inflation as measured by the increase in the consumer price index.
(b) Real rates are calculated by subtracting from the nominal rate the geometric average of the rate of inflation in the current year and the next year. Figures for 1986 are thus estimates.
Authors' calculations from the same source, table A9.

tion of the rates of inflation – which is partially done in rows (b) of the same table – both the levels of the real rate of interest during the whole period and their rates of change in 1981, at the start of the period under study, are greatly increased. Whatever the measure, though, the real rate is higher on average in the USA than in Europe.

A stylized fact can thus be enunciated: in the 1980s real interest rates have been abnormally high around the world, with a positive differential having developed between US and European rates.

2.3 User Cost of Capital

In 1981 the United States Congress enacted investment subsidies mainly in the form of a drastic reduction of the fiscal life of capital equipment, which has led to a corresponding increase of fiscal depreciation allowances. As a consequence direct corporate taxation as a percentage of GDP has decreased considerably. (The previous decrease is due to the reduction of the rate of corporate income tax legislated in 1979). This was not the case for the European countries, where no similar change occurred in the 1980s.

The effect of the legislation is even more striking if one looks at the evolution of the user cost of capital. Figures 2.3a–c depict the evolution for three countries: France, the FRG and the USA.[2] By themselves these evolutions are interesting and reflect rather well the effect of increasing real rates of interest on the

[19]

user cost of capital. But what should be underlined is the fact that, for the first time, in 1981–82, the after-tax user cost of capital in the USA is lower than the gross-of-tax user cost. In the two other countries there is no indication of a narrowing between the two curves.

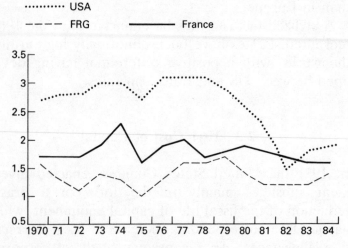

FIGURE 2.1 Direct corporate taxes (percentage of GDP)

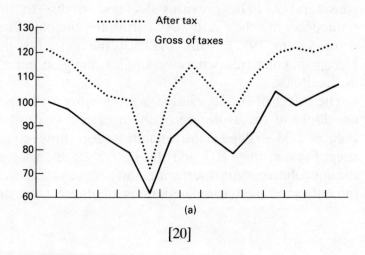

(a)

[20]

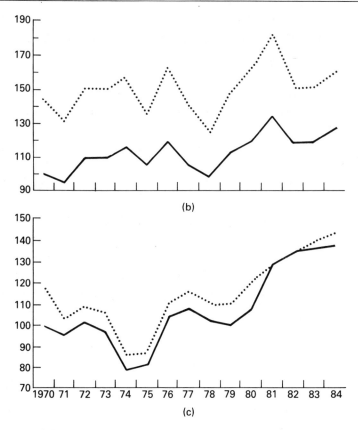

FIGURE 2.2   User cost of capital: (a) France, (b) FRG, (c) USA

2.4   Wage Shares

The increase in the real interest rates was then not compensated by any fiscal alleviation in Europe. In addition, rates of taxation and social contribution have actually increased there – and have led to a decrease

[21]

in the profitability of European firms. The latter will be restored if some compensatory change in the share of profit (wage) occurs.

There was no clear trend in the wage share in the 1970s in the USA, while in Europe it was increasing in most countries. In contrast, from 1980 to 1985 the share of wages in value added has decreased almost everywhere – an exception being Italy – but much more in Europe than in the USA where the decrease is negligible. The percentage changes during the periods 1971–80 and 1981–85 of the wage share for the whole economy are given in table 2.3.

TABLE 2.3   Rate of change of the wage share in Europe and in the USA, 1971–80 and 1981–85

Periods	USA	France	FRG	Italy	UK	Europe (12)
1971–80	0.1	6.5	0.7	1.2	2.7	2
1981–85	−0.1	−2.5	−5.8	0.9	−2.4	−3.9

Source: Authors' calculations from European Economy, no. 29, July 1986, table 24.

These evolutions reflect the combined effect of the patterns of real (product) wages and labor productivity. In the 1980s the rate of increase of both product and real wages has slowed down in Europe as compared to the 1970s.

We shall argue in chapter 4 that the rise in Europe of the share going to profit reflects the workings of competition in customer markets. Through the exchange rate, and the increase of real interest rates, the foreign disturbances of the early 1980s have induced European firms to push up their mark-ups.

2.5 Mark-ups

A significant piece of evidence that this increase in Europe's mark-up relative to America's occurred – taking into account the trend in both regions – is the stylized fact we have established *à propos* exchange rates movements. The third column of table 2.1 for each European country shows the disparity between the evolutions of European and US mark-ups, and the relative increase of Europe's mark-up in the first half of the 1980s.

Figures 2.3a–e give direct evidence of these divergent evolutions.[3] Two important points emerge:

1 During the 1970s, when the dollar was depreciating against the European currencies (see table 2.1) and when the real interest rates were low and decreasing, the mark-ups were characterized typically by an increasing trend in the USA and a decreasing trend in the four European countries considered.

2 During the 1980s real appreciation of the dollar and high levels of real interest rates combined in such a way that on average the mark-up in the USA was slightly above its 1970–80 trend (below the trend until the beginning of 1983 and well above after); while in Europe, in the first half of

[23]

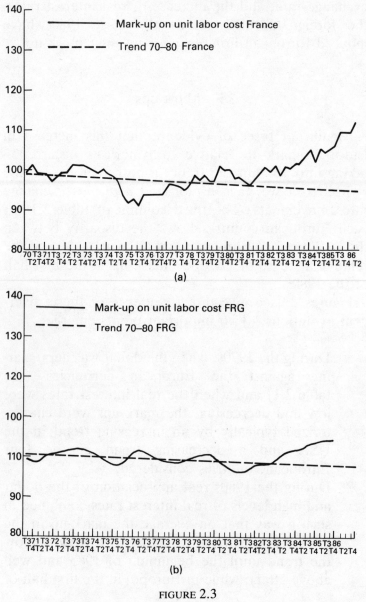

FIGURE 2.3

[24]

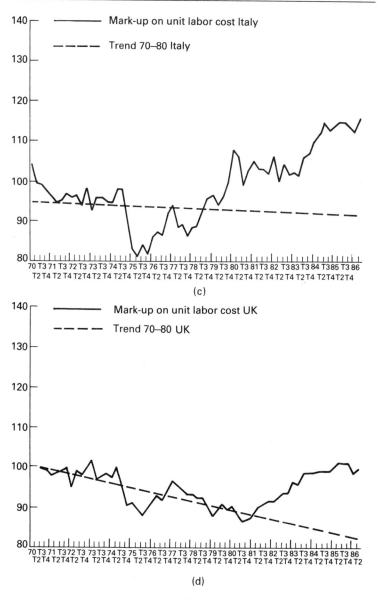

(c)

(d)

FIGURE 2.3   cont.

[25]

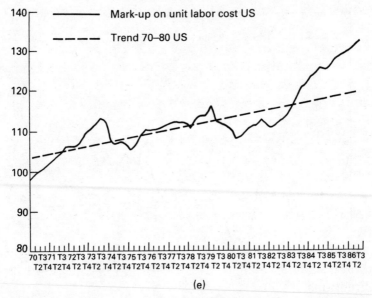

(e)

FIGURE 2.3 Departure of the price-unit labor cost mark-up from its 1970–80 trend: (a) France, (b) FRG, (c) Italy, (d) UK, (e) USA

* The mark-up is measured as the ratio of the GDP deflator to unit labor cost in manufacturing. (*Source*: author's calculations using data from the US Bureau of Labor Statistics and from the OECD. The new revised series on unit labor cost have been used.)

the 1980s, mark-ups are generally well above their 1970–80 trend, the departure in percentage of the trend's values being much greater than in the USA. This statement has to be qualified for the FRG where the picture is very similar to that of the USA.

We shall argue in chapter 4 that the sharp elevation of actual and, presumably, of expected real interest rates (see table 2.2) induced firms in Europe to widen

[26]

their mark-ups since it increased the opportunity cost of investing in greater or maintained market share through restraint in present prices at a sacrifice in present cash flow. The same effect applies to US firms. But the consequence of the real appreciation of the dollar is an implied gain of competitiveness for European firms. That windfall gain induces the European firms to widen their mark-ups and thus to slow the prospective rise in their market share. Conversely it induces the US firms, to shave their mark-ups and thus to moderate the prospective erosion of their market share. Hence the two forces – real interest rates and real exchange rates – both pulled the European mark-up in the same upward direction, but pulled the US mark-up in opposite directions.

2.6 Average Product of Labor

Everywhere, in Europe as in the USA, productivity speeded up from 1982 (1980 for the UK). The productivity cycle has been on average shorter and less pronounced in the 1980s than it was following the first oil shock. Not only has average labor productivity decreased less than previously during the recession phase, but it has resumed its past trend much earlier than in the 1970s. For example, after a sharp fall in 1974 (2.5 percent), it took more than 2 years for productivity to reach its 1973 level in the USA again. But in 1982 productivity fell only by 0.5 percent and in 1983 it was already two percentage points higher than its 1981 level. Similar stories may be told for most European countries. What is even more striking is the fact that in Europe productivity recovered generally when the economy was still mired in a slump. This difference between the 1970s and the 1980s, we will argue in chapter 4, reflects faster dishoarding of labor in the latter period induced by the higher real rate of interest.

2.7 Investment

The behavior of investment fits the general picture. Investment in capital goods (machines and equipment) was generally lower than its peak level of 1979 until 1983. In 1984 it has about resumed in Europe its 1979 level, but in the USA is about 20 percent higher. Hence investment is well below the trend in Europe and likely a little above in the USA (see figure 2.5).

The same behavior has characterized all kinds of investments. On average, during the first half of the 1980s, gross fixed capital formation has exhibited a zero growth rate in the European countries. As a consequence its share in gross domestic product has steadily declined. This is in contrast to the USA, where by 1985 the share of gross fixed capital formation in GDP has resumed its average value of the 1970s (see table 2.4).

We will argue in chapters 4 and 6 that the resulting decline of the capital stock in Europe, relative to the past trend, has acted as a supply shock that exerts a cumulative contractionary influence on employment.

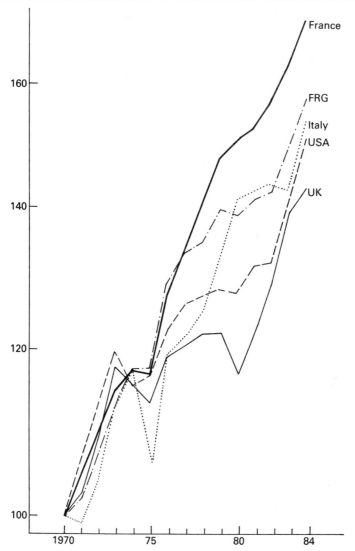

FIGURE 2.4 Average labor productivity in the manufacturing
sector
(*Source*: OECD)

[29]

TABLE 2.4 Gross fixed capital formation in Europe and in the USA

Periods	France		FRG		Italy		UK		Europe (12)		USA	
	Share of GDP	Rate of change	Share of GDP	Rate of change	Share of GDP	Rate of change	Share of GDP	Rate of change	Share of GDP	Rate of change	Share of GDP	Rate of change
1971–1980*	22.9	2.9	22.3	1.4	20.1	1.1	19.2	0.4	21.5	1.6	18.4	2.4
1981	21.4	−1.1	21.8	−4.8	20.2	0.6	16.4	−9.4	20.2	−4.1	17.8	1.1
1982	20.8	0.7	20.5	−5.3	19	−5.2	16.4	6.4	19.5	−1.5	16.5	−6.6
1983	19.8	−2.3	20.6	3.2	18	−3.8	16.4	4.6	18.9	−0.4	16.8	8.1
1984	18.9	−2.2	20.3	0.8	17.9	4.1	17.4	8.2	18.6	1.3	17.9	18
1985	18.8	3	19.7	−0.3	17.9	4.1	17	1	18.5	2.3	18.4	7.3

* Average yearly rate of change.
Source: European Economy, no. 29, July 1986, tables 14 and 15.

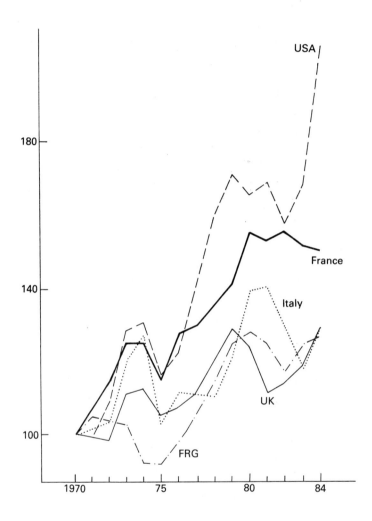

FIGURE 2.5 Investment in capital goods
(*Source*: OECD, *Quarterly National Accounts*, various issues).

[31]

2.8   Relative Price of Capital Goods

It can be deduced from the above stylized facts that world investment fell during the period under consideration, although its diminution has not been evenly distributed. If we assume that, especially in Europe, automatic fiscal stabilizers and transfer payments affect primarily consumption expenditures, it could then be deduced that the relative price of newly produced capital goods should fall. This is exactly what happens everywhere, though with somewhat different intensities.

The relative price of capital good (machines and equipment) has fallen in the USA as well as in Europe from 1979. As a general proposition the extent of the fall, relative to trend has been greater in the USA than in Europe.

We shall argue in chapter 4 that the decline in the relative world price of capital goods was attributable

TABLE 2.5   Real price of investment goods, Europe and the USA, 1981–85 percentage deviation from 1970–80 trend values

Country	1981	1982	1983	1984	1985
France	−3.82	−4.46	−6.46	−7.36	−9.03
FRG	−0.43	−0.20	−0.10	n.a.	n.a.
Italy	−7.45	−10.67	−13.88	n.a.	n.a.
UK	−6.98	−7.99	−7.98	−7.65	−6.35
USA	−5.78	−8.73	−11.03	−14.05	−17.28

Source: authors' calculations using data from OECD, National Accounts, 1972–84, vol. 2, Detailed Tables, and Quarterly National Accounts, various issues.

to the disturbances in US economic policies and that, in combination with wage indexation, the implication was a contraction of aggregate employment in Europe.

2.9 (Un)employment

The above evolutions had strong but contrasting consequences for the pattern of employment in Europe and the USA. Unemployment has been steadily increasing since the first oil shock in Europe, but at a higher rate since 1979. In contrast, despite the major recession of 1981–82, the rate of increase of unemployment in the USA has been three times lower in the 1980–84 period than in the period following the first oil shock. These trends reflect a contrasting evolution, as the unemployment rate has actually decreased in America since 1982 and there is not a

TABLE 2.6   Net job creations (yearly average, in thousands)

Country	1964–73	1974–80	1981–84	1964–84
France	160	71	−100	81
Italy	−90	171	25	19
FRG	20	−86	−250	−67
UK	40	29	−325	−33
EEC	200	270	−650	62
USA	1700	2014	1450	1762

Source: M. Anyadike-Danes and J.-P. Fitoussi, "Dimensions du problème de l'emploi en Europe et aux Etats-Unis", Lettre de l'OFCE, no. 12, February 1984.

[33]

single year where it did so in Europe until the bumpy recovery that began in the FRG, UK and Italy in 1986.

Moreover, the increase in unemployment in Europe in the 1970s has not the same meaning as its rise in the first half of the 1980s.[4] Between 1974 and 1980, on average, the annual net creation of jobs in Europe was higher than during the previous period of rapid growth of GNP (1964–73). In contrast, in the 1981–84 period, employment increased by 5,800,000 in the USA and *decreased* by 2,600,000 in the EEC. (It should be borne in mind that the size of the labor force is about the same in both regions.)

Notes

1 The conventionally measured long-term real rate of interest is defined as the nominal long-term interest rate less the percentage change in the CPI during the previous 12 months.
2 The series have been calculated using normal assumption by A. Gubian, F. Guillaumat-Tailliet, and J. Le Cacheux: "Fiscalité des entreprises et décision d'investissement," *Observations et Diagnostics Economiques*, no. 16, July 1986.
3 The measure of the price mark-up on unit labor cost is imperfect, as the new revised series on unit labor cost are available for the manufacturing sector only. Two price indices have been tried, the GDP deflator and the index of consumer prices. Fortunately the general evolutions are the same with both.
4 During the two periods the annual rate of increase of the labor force is about the same.

3

Orthodox Theory

The three mechanisms that are central to our explanation of how the US shocks in the 1980s brought a slump to Europe – the mark-up in customer markets, the contractual or indexed behavior of wages, and the cost and other supply effects of real interest rates – can be said (with little or no exaggeration) to be novel to the macroeconomic analysis of slumps such as the recent one in Europe. But are these new theoretical wrinkles necessary to understand the European slump? It may be wondered whether we are simply putting old wine in new bottles. To show that models containing these novel mechanisms cast the influence of the US disturbances upon Europe in a new light we need first to review present-day orthodox theory concerning the transmission of foreign shocks. In this review we will be led to rewrite the standard model along more aggregative lines, with emphasis on investment theory, in order to tailor it to questions of interdependence between two very large and quite similar nations or currency unions of nations.

[35]

3.1　The Standard Propositions and Qualifications

The existing theoretical literature on interdependence has been confined to the construction and analysis of two-country models, and this conception of the world seems good enough for our purposes here. We shall associate the "foreign country" with the USA and the "home country" we may interpret as "Europe," more precisely, the collection of (mostly European) countries tied by more-or-less fixed exchange rates to one another, a group which includes (at least) the nations in the EMS.

The orthodox theory grew out of the conceptions of international trade and the world capital market found in the Mundell–Fleming one-country model (1962, 1963). The extension to two countries was first made by Robert Mundell in 1964. The theory is well expounded in the definitive manual by Rudiger Dornbusch in 1980.[1] In these models one of the countries specializes in Ricardo's cloth, say, and the other country in Ricardo's wine, though both may be on a super-power scale. There is perfect "capital mobility" which meant that the real rate of interest (in cloth or wine) is the same across borders, though in practice it was assumed that the same equalization applied also to the nominal interest rates (defined with reference to the two national currencies, respectively). Two exchange rate regimes are explored in this literature, that of a fixed exchange rate and that of a fluctuating rate under a monetarist policy of fixed national money supplies.

[36]

In the (latter) fluctuating-rate monetarist case, which is the case more nearly descriptive of the behavior of the exchange rate between the dollar and the European currencies in the period of our study, 1981–85, two remarkably definite conclusions are drawn by the orthodox theory with regard to international interdependence: *tight money abroad* – that is, a contraction of the money supply in the foreign country – tends to *increase* aggregate employment in the *home* country while (not surprisingly) it decreases employment in the foreign country. *Fiscal stimulus abroad* – say, a general tax cut on personal incomes that acts to boost consumer demand abroad – serves also to *increase* employment in the *home* country while it increases employment in the foreign country as well. (Only if the latter country is a small producer in the world would it suffer the small-country fate of seeing the part of its increased consumer demand that falls on its own output merely "crowd out" a virtually equal amount of exports, so that the rest of the world receives virtually the whole stimulus.)

The first of these conclusions, the beneficence of tight money abroad, is obtained by arguing that if employment, and hence the demand for money, in the home country did *not* increase, so that the interest rate was left unchanged, it would find its interest rate below the new level to which tight money abroad has driven up the interest rate in the foreign country; so the home country's currency must depreciate until output and thus the demand for money at home have risen sufficiently to pull up the interest rate to the level abroad. It is perfectly true in these orthodox models

[37]

that the stipulated increase of the interest rate and fall of real income in the foreign country will have *some* contractionary effects upon the home country. However, in the crisp summary of Dornbusch, "The contractionary effects of higher interest rate and lower income [abroad] are more than offset by the depreciation of the [home] currency" (1980, p. 201). This must be the result because the rise of the nominal interest rate at home necessarily spurs the velocity of the home country's money supply.

The expansionary effect of the foreign fiscal stimulus on the home country is equally unambiguous in the orthodox theory. This conclusion too is attributable to the result that the foreign interest rate rises and the hypothesis of nominal interest rate equalization across borders. The implied rise in the interest rate at home reduces the amount of money demanded, freeing idle cash balances and thus boosting "velocity," so that the unchanged money supply will support a higher level of output and real income, which is accomplished via the requisite depreciation of the home currency.

Two extensions of the orthodox model that require some qualification of the above conclusions must be mentioned. Recent mathematical treatments of two-country interdependence admit the possibility that one or both countries import the good produced abroad for use as an input, or intermediate good, as well as a final good for consumption.[2] Consequently, tight money abroad, by curtailing production of the foreign good, and foreign fiscal stimulus, in so far as it tilts world demand toward the foreign good, raise the relative price of the foreign good; this "real deprecia-tion" of the home country currency will decrease the supply of home-good output while increasing the demand. In principle this supply effect could outweigh the demand effect, leaving a net *contraction* of home output.

A somewhat parallel qualification can result if the calculation of the "real cash balances" for which consumers have a demand uses the consumer price index as the deflator. It may be, then, that the real depreciation caused by the foreign monetary or fiscal disturbance will generate an excess demand for real cash balances (output constant) by decreasing the real supply, since the home price of the foreign good will be driven up.[3] If that is the case, the home country depreciation re-establishing interest rate equality tends not only to increase the demand for real cash balances by increasing output and thus real income, but also tends to decrease the supply of real balances, which reduces the level of real balances demanded that is required to achieve the new interest rate. It is theoretically possible that this real balance effect could alone achieve interest rate equality, with no increase of output or even a net *contraction* of output.[4]

Although these qualifications are very welcome – we too wish to argue that the American shocks contracted output and employment in Europe, contrary to the orthodox presumption – as an empirical matter these complications do not appear to have much importance for economic relations between the USA and Europe. When Michael Bruno and Jeffrey Sachs lean toward assigning these factors appreciable weight we do not

[39]

quarrel with their instinct: *cherchez le "supply"*. But we consider these particular supply effects to be weak reeds on which to build a counter-model of the transmission of shocks between the USA and Europe.[5] In these two regions we have largely the same list of goods produced and in not greatly different proportions. Hence, from a classical stand-point, there is no reason to expect much trade between them; we should expect that most of Europe's trade is intra-European, and likewise most US "trade" is with itself. There *is* reason, on the other hand, to expect some trans-Atlantic trade to occur out of the happenstance of customer relations. In fact, there has been observed to be a significant *two-way* trade in the majority of manufacturing items in the USA and in European countries. Nor does it appear that Europe makes heavy use of US output as intermediate goods. The input contributed to Europe's gross product by US cotton, sugar, soymeal, oil, and so forth, does not seem important enough to merit a major part in a theory of the slump in Europe. In fact the 1980s tell a story of collapsing real prices of raw materials, not steeper prices.[6]

3.2 The Essential Orthodox Model

Since the USA and Europe are so alike in technology, resources and tastes it is not unreasonable to proceed in the opposite direction of discarding the whole Ricardian notion of innate comparative advantage. We can reduce the orthodox analysis (with its characteristic premise of perfect markets) to its essentials, and also smooth the way for consideration of our own highly aggregative models, by supposing instead, purely for convenience, that the two countries produce the *same good*. (Later, in one of our own models, we shall suppose they produce the same consumer good and the same capital good, though the market for the former will be imperfect.) We shall see that nothing is lost in this simplification of the orthodox theory of the international transmission of foreign monetary and fiscal disturbances, and much clarity is gained.

The essential aggregative orthodox model is described by the following six-equation system:

$$(WAD) \quad Z+Z^* = G_o+G^*_o+C_o+C^*_o+ I(r^e,Z^e)+I^*(r^e,Z^{*e}) \tag{1}$$

$$(LOP) \quad P^* = E^*P(= E^{-1}P) \tag{2}$$

$$(SS) \quad Z = Z^s(P/W, K_{-1}), \quad W/W_o = (P/P_o)^u \tag{3}$$

$$(SS^*) \quad Z^* = Z^{s*}(P^*/W^*, K^*_{-1}), \quad W^*/W^*_o = (P^*/P^*_o)^{u^*} \tag{4}$$

$$(LM) \quad M_o = PL(PZ/P, r^e+\dot{p}^e) \tag{5}$$

$$(LM^*) \quad M^*_o = P^* L^* (P^* Z^*/P^*, r^e + \dot{p}^e + \dot{x}^{*e}) \tag{6}$$

where: r^e = worldwide expected real rate of interest

Z = home country output level

P = home-country price level, P_o in the base year

[41]

E	= home country price of foreign exchange
W	= the home wage level, W_o in the base year
G	= output purchased by the home government
C	= consumer purchases by home residents
M	= home money supply
Z^e	= present-period expectation of next-period Z
$\dot{p}^e$	= expected rate of inflation
$\dot{x}^e$	= expected rate of home-currency depreciation

and where the foreign-country variables and parameters, Z^*, E^*, x^{*e} and so on, are defined correspondingly. The subscript o after a variable signifies that it is predetermined by history, or that the variable is held constant by government policy absent a shift of policy. Here and below all coefficients, such as u in the present model, are non-negative.

This is a discrete-time model, though not one requiring regularity in the length of the successive periods. The present period is best conceived as running 3 or 4 years, corresponding to the years 1982–85. In a period of such length the (negative) diminishing-return effect of the volume of investment on the one-period rate of return, given the level of output next period, is non-negligible in principle (though perhaps small enough to be unimportant). Inverting, we find domestic investment, I, to be decreasing in the rate of return and increasing in future output. By supposing, as is conventional, that firms invest just enough to equate their expectations of the rate of return, which is a function of expected future output, to the worldwide expected real interest rate (common to both countries,[7] we are led to the national aggregate demand relation $C_o + G_o + I(r^e, Z^e)$ and to equation (1) which describes world aggregate demand (WAD).

The remaining equations are straightforward. Equation (2) expresses the law of one price (*LOP*). Equations (3) and (4) describe the upward-sloping competitive supply curves in the two countries. To obtain the wage here we suppose either that money wage rates are sluggish, so W is essentially predetermined at the level W_o, for example, or else indexed to the price level with an indexation-elasticity coefficient, u at home and u^* abroad, between zero and one (an elasticity of one is excluded here). Hence the amount of output supplied is always an increasing function of price despite possible wage indexation. Equations (5) and (6) contain the *LM* relations. Note that the second argument of the L function is the home nominal interest rate, i, and the second argument of L^* is similarly the foreign nominal interest rate, i^*, since $i^* = i + \dot{x}^{*e}$, which is the fundamental interest-rate parity principle. (Lenders add to the external interest rate their expectation of the rate of depreciation of their own currency to obtain the interest rate they require on internal loans.)

The behavior of the modeled economy in response to our foreign monetary and fiscal shocks can be

[43]

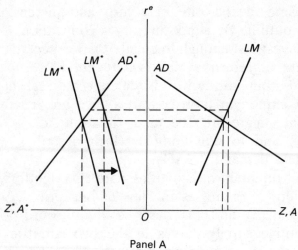

Panel A

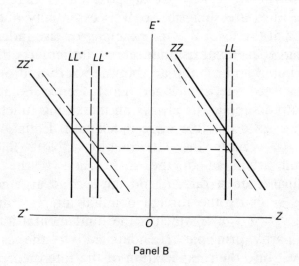

Panel B

FIGURE 3.1   An aggregate orthodox model

[44]

illustrated by either of the back-to-back pairs of diagrams in figure 3.1. In panel A, which has some obvious parallels to the *IS–LM* diagram by Hicks, the right-hand diagram refers to home, the left-hand one to the foreign country. The curve *AD* shows how real national *expenditure, A,* by the home country, $C_o + G_o + I$, decreases with r^e, given Z^e, while the familiar *LM* curve shows how the one-period real interest rate, given the expected inflation rate, increases with national output. The underlying equations are:

$$(AD) \quad A = G_o + C_o + I(r^e, Z^e)$$
$$(LM) \quad M_o = P^s \, (Z/K_{-1}, W_o/P^u_o) \, L(Z, r^e + \dot{p}^e)$$

where the supply price function P^s is an inversion of *SS*. The curves *AD** and *LM** are correspondingly defined. Clearly, expenditure may be greater or less than output; but world expenditure must equal world output. So, in equilibrium, one country's excess-supply-like lateral discrepancy between its curves must be counterbalanced by an opposite excess-demand-like gap in the other country.

A foreign tight-money disturbance is described by an inward shift of the *LM** curve in panel A. The implication, holding the expectational parameters constant for a moment, is that r^e rises until the excess of output over expenditure in the home country has been pushed up, and the excess of expenditure over output abroad has been pushed down, to the point where the gaps are equal. Clearly this rise of the interest rate implies in turn an *expansion* of *home* output through its effect on the velocity of money.

[45]

(The induced fall of expenditure at home and abroad can only dampen the rise of r^e and thus moderate the expansion of home output and magnify the contraction of foreign output.)

A foreign fiscal disturbance in the shape of a boost to C^*_0 causes an upward, hence outward, shift of AD^* (this shift is not drawn). Expectational parameters constant, the implication is again a rise of r^e until the *expansion* of output at home and abroad, operating through its effect on velocity, has brought world output up to the increased level of world expenditure. Note that this disturbance, taken alone, has no unambiguous implications for the exchange rate. In contrast, the monetary disturbance implies an appreciation of the foreign currency, since it is through an appreciation that foreign output is forced to fall.

An investment subsidy instituted abroad can be seen to have the same consequences; but its effects upon the real interest rate are larger.

For another perspective readers may want to refer to the viewpoint taken in panel B of figure 3.1 where it is the real interest rate that is in the background rather than the exchange rate. Note first that, given a level of world output demand, denoted by $Z^0 + Z^{*0}$, P and Z will be decreasing functions while P^* and Z^* will be increasing functions of the value of the home currency, E^*. (This is a straightforward two-country supply–demand exercise not shown here.) Given r^e as well as the expectational parameters, therefore, which thus fixes the amount of world output demanded according to equation (1), there is a negative relationship between E^* and Z, which is depicted by the ZZ

curve in the right-hand diagram of panel B in figure 3.1. The *LM* equation, on the other hand, gives another relationship between *E* and *Z*, which is the curve *LL*. Since *LL* determines the real value of cash balances through the supply price of output regarded as a function of *Z*, it is a vertical line. The underlying equations are:

$$(ZZ) \quad Z = Z^s \, [P(E^*, Z^0 + Z^{*0}, W_o, W^*_o)^{1-u}/ \\ W_o \, P_o^{-u}, \, K_{-1}]$$
$$(LL) \quad M_o = P^s(Z/K_{-1}, W_o/P_o^u) \, L(Z, r^e + \dot{p}^e)$$

The curves ZZ^* and LL^* in the left-hand diagram of panel B are correspondingly defined. In these back-to-back diagrams all the curves refer to output, none to expenditure, so there must be simultaneous intersections in equilibrium.

A foreign tight-money disturbance shifts inward the LL^* schedule in panel B. From the standpoint of the left-hand figure the implication is a fall of E^* (an appreciation of the foreign currency) while no disturbance to the intersections occurs in the right-hand figure. To reconcile the disparate intersection ordinates there must be a rise of r^e. That will shift ZZ down and ZZ^* up, and it will shift both LL and LL^* out, all moves serving to bring the intersections into line at the same exchange rate.

A foreign tax cut boosting C^*_o causes both ZZ and ZZ^* to shift outward, so that a rise of r^e is again required to bring the intersections back into line. E^* could be left higher or lower.

A foreign investment subsidy can be seen to have

qualitatively similar effects, raising r^e and Z whether or not E as well.

Before we leave the orthodox theory we need to tie up loose ends with two points about dynamic expectations. The first observation concerns the expected future output levels. Suppose that in each country there is a tendency for any output fluctuation to persist in some damped fashion owing to an incomplete tendency of wages to restore the normal level of employment. Then the fall of Z^* resulting from the tight-money shock will be accompanied by a fall of Z^{*e}. Consequently the AD^* schedule, which takes Z^{*e} as given, will shift down by an amount related to the fall of Z^*. The result is a lessening or even a reversal of the rise of r^e. (It is a familiar feature of Tobin–Sargent type models that the real interest rate falls when employment and thus capital utilization rates fall.) It is theoretically possible, therefore, that tight money abroad will fail to expand output at home or will even contract it.[8] But, of course, tight money abroad accompanied by a foreign fiscal stimulus that leaves foreign output unchanged on balance *would* unambiguously raise the real interest rate, since both AD^* and LM^* are then shifted up in the left-hand figure of panel A of figure 3.1. This *package* of foreign disturbances *would* thus lead to an expansion of home output. Since we may safely presume that the package of US policies pulled up the expected real interest rate in the 1980s, the above qualification regarding expected future output is not crucial. So the orthodox theory does not escape its uncomfortable implications this way.

[48]

The second observation concerns the expected rates of inflation – the expected rate of change of E^*P abroad, and the expected rate of change of EP^* at home. It might be suspected that these expectations may behave so as to overturn the foregoing implications of the orthodox model. Maybe foreign tight money, in causing a big slump abroad, generates expected (further) deflation abroad (because P^* is believed to "undershoot" this period) or expected depreciation abroad (because E is believed to "overshoot" this period) so that there is expected deflation at home, and this effect is *strong* enough that output is *contracted* on balance by the foreign tight money. A full formal analysis is beyond the modest purposes of this review of orthodoxy, but we may argue against such an outcome as follows (making limited appeal to correct foresight). Suppose that in each country there is at least *some* tendency for nominal wage rates (or rewritten wage contracts) to restore employment next period to the normal pre-shock level. If, following a monetary shock, there is an understood tendency for reversion to the normal, it will be expected that EP^*, which has presumably deviated from the normal this period, will move part-way (or all the way) back to normal next period. Hence there can either be an *elevation* of EP^* and therefore P this period, together with expected *deflation* (next period), or a *fall* of EP^* and P this period accompanied by expected *inflation*, that is, the expected (partial or full) recovery of P. But the latter is a theoretical impossibility: It implies that the nominal interest rate (i) is unambiguously higher, both because of the higher r^e owing to tight money and because of the expected inflation, which implies (via *LM*) a rise of output and hence (via *SS*) a *rise* of *P* this period, which is a contradiction. Thus orthodox theory inescapably implies that if r^e is driven up by a foreign monetary tightening, EP^* and therefore *P* and *Z* must rise – with P^* undershooting or *E* overshooting or both – with EP^* and *P* expected to recede next period. The expected deflation is the result of the momentary elevation of *P*, not a source of lower *P* and *Z*.

Notes

1 R. A. Mundell, "Capital mobility and stabilization policy under fixed and flexible exchange rates," *Canadian Journal of Economics and Political Science*, November 1963, with appendix. R. A. Mundell, "A reply: capital mobility and size," *Canadian Journal of Economics and Political Science*, vol. 30, August 1964. R. Dornbusch, *Open-Economy Macro-economics*, New York: Basic Books, 1980, chapter 11.

2 Hence the amount of home country output, denoted by *Z*, that home producers wish to supply is some function Z^S of the real (or relative) price of the foreign good as well as the price of the home good in wage units (which is the reciprocal of the product wage) and the predetermined capital stock: $Z = Z^S$ (P/W, EP^*/P, K_{-1}). Here *P* is the home-good price, P^* the foreign-good price abroad, and EP^* the home price of the foreign good.

3 Let P^C denote the consumer price index, a function of *P* and EP^*. In these terms the money demand function might be $M = P^C L(PY/P^C, i)$. Note that the excess demand for money is an increasing function of P^C *only if* the real-income elasticity of *L* is less than one.

4 Both of these complications are rigorously analyzed in an

admirable paper by B. Daniel, "The international transmission of economic disturbances under flexible exchange rates," *International Economic Review*, vol. 22, October 1981, 491–509. Yet so many complexities have been introduced all at once that it is not easy for the reader to be completely clear about the effects of any one of them.

5   M. Bruno and J. D. Sachs, *Economics of Worldwide Stagflation*.

6   See Rudiger Dornbusch, "Policy and performance links between LDC debtors and industrial nations," Brookings Papers on Economic Activity, 1985, no. 2.

7   It can be argued as follows that there will not be different expected real rates of interest in the two countries. From the interest–parity relation between nominal rates, $i = i^* + \dot{E}^e/E$, we have $r^e = i^* - (\dot{P}^*/P^*)^e + (\dot{E}/E) + (\dot{P}/P)^e - (\dot{P}^*/P^*)^e$. But the right-hand side is equal to r^{*e} if $P^e = E^e P^{*e}$ as well as $P = EP^*$.

8   The latter case implies that the fall of foreign output induces a fall of investment expenditure by foreign firms that exceeds the fall of output, which means that "*IS*" has the "wrong" slope.

[51]

4

Elements of a Reconstructed Theory

Our explanation of the 1980s slump in Europe finds the principal source, or at any rate a major source, in the fiscal and monetary shocks originating in the USA in the first few years of this decade. These foreign disturbances were the policy shift toward tighter money taken by the Federal Reserve in early 1981; the three-stage reduction of tax rates on personal incomes known as the Reagan tax cut beginning in 1982; and the investment subsidies, or tax relief, enacted by the Congress in 1981 (and modified in 1982). The latter measures were largely scaled back or eliminated in 1986.

We argue that, taken together whether or not taken singly, these shocks acted to drive up the dollar and real interest rates in Europe; through these exchange rate and interest rate channels the US shocks had impacts in Europe upon mark-ups in customer markets, the real price of investment-goods output, and various kinds of investment expenditure; these impacts had in turn serious repercussions for European employment and output.

[53]

1   European firms operating in customer markets were doubly tempted to push up their mark-ups. Taking advantage of the increased competitiveness brought by currency depreciation, they sought somewhat higher prices for the same outputs in order to increase their profits in the present, rather than resting content with the whole gain in the form of increased market share and increased profit in the future. This induced push of mark-ups increased the demand for money at given total employment and in so doing contracted aggregate output and employment (in the same way that a decreased money supply has such effects). In addition, firms raised mark-ups again in response to the elevation of real interest rates (while in the USA this effect merely countered the fall of mark-ups due to dollar appreciation). The upward push of the price index of consumer goods (at a given output) clashed with contractual or indexed wages, forcing a fall of output and employment on this score as well.

2   Firms reacted to higher real rates of interest by disinvesting in their "hoards" of human capital, i.e. by dishoarding employees, and more gradually by disinvesting in plant and equipment as such capital wore out. The former effect tended to produce accelerated retirement of workers rather than re-employment at new firms, thus a fall of employment.[1] The latter effects, besides its obvious consequence for output, may have driven up marginal costs enough to force a

[54]

decline of employment as well. This result is more nearly assured the fuller the degree of wage indexation.

3   Although the last of the US policy shocks may ultimately have restored US investment expenditure to its trend level, an effect of the shocks taken together was to reduce world investment expenditure through a higher real interest rate, and thus reduce investment-goods output in Europe at least, while consumer expenditure around the world was more robust. As a consequence, if its total employment were not to change, Europe would have to see increased employment in its consumer-good sector to offset reduced employment in the capital-goods sector, and this resource reallocation would mean that the price level (in local currency) in the consumer-goods sector would have to rise while the price of capital goods fell (provided there cannot be so large a reallocation of "shiftable" capital from capital-goods making to consumer-goods making as to overturn this Marshallian presumption). But a higher consumer-good price level entails higher indexed or contractual wages, an effect which acts to reduce aggregate output and employment; indexation (full or not) in wage arrangements prevents the full decline of the "product wage" in the consumer-goods industries needed to counterbalance the original increase of the product wage in the capital-goods industries.

[55]

We shall not attempt to argue that every one of the policy shocks emanating from the USA spelled a contraction of both output and employment, though such a result may have been the case. But it will be argued that the *package* of policy innovations, by raising the real interest rate in Europe and lowering the real value of the European currencies, had predominantly contractionary effects upon both employment and output in Europe over the five year period under study, 1981 to 1985. (It might be, for example, that the beneficial demand effect of the investment subsidies upon Europe exceeded the deleterious supply effect, while the tight money had also an adverse supply effect upon Europe and an adverse demand effect that can be shown to cancel or exceed the aforementioned demand effect, which leaves a negative net effect of the two shocks taken together.)

4.1 Customer Markets in the Transmission of Foreign Shocks

In considering the slump in Europe our strategy will be to make a series of departures from the orthodox model, each in a new theoretical direction, always returning to the orthodox base camp for the next excursion rather than attempting to accumulate the departures as we go.

Our introduction of customer markets, while perhaps the most radical, involves few alterations of the orthodox model in the extremely aggregative case – and so we present it first.

[56]

A useful simplification will be made here and in the discussions of the other innovations proposed below. As we saw earlier, the whole emphasis of the orthodox transmission theory is on the rate of interest: if it rises (falls) the velocity of money is increased (decreased) and the monetary authorities, being strict monetarists, watch passively as the velocity change disturbs output and employment in the same direction. Such strict monetarism is possibly a reference point from which the monetary authorities may decide to deviate (or not to deviate) in response to the disturbance. But it might make equal or greater sense to suppose that the authorities are inclined to a sort of *liberal monetarism*: they tend ordinarily to "accommodate" a fall of interest rates and to "offset" rises, thus stabilizing "MV" more nearly than M. In any case, we shall follow other authors in adopting this convenient reformulation.[2]

The key feature of customer markets is that, owing to informational frictions in the movement of buyers over supplying firms, industry price is not competed down to the perfectly competitive supply price, which is marginal cost, except under a zero real rate of interest. A firm's mark-up policy makes its price an increasing function of the price (known or expected) at the other firms, its marginal cost level, and the (expected) real interest rate.[3] The elasticities with respect to the first two factors add up to one. Hence the supply price (at a given output) of the firms in a country will be pushed up by a rise in the price (expressed in the same currency) charged by foreign firms, though less than equiproportionately; equiva-

[57]

lently, the amount supplied (at a given price) will be pulled down by a rise in the foreign price, though an equiproportionate increase of the own price would have a larger proportionate effect (in the opposite direction).

In modelling the demand side we have chosen a rather extreme case to expedite exposition: Foreign firms initially have all the foreign customers – consumers and purchasers of investment goods alike – and the home firms initially have all the home-based customers. This is the case in the present period, though not generally next period, as customers perceive and respond to price differences across borders. Note that if firms cannot distinguish between consumers and "investors," the relative price of investment goods will be intertemporally constant and thus not intrude into real interest rates and real income.

Finally we introduce the liberal-monetarist policy which makes the supply of money the same function of the interest rate as the demand for money. Replacing M_o by the pre-accommodation money supply, M'_o, thus produces an LM' equation lacking the interest rate.

These new features lead to the following extreme case (descriptive in the initial period) of an aggregative customer-market model.

$$(ZZ) \quad Z = G_o + C_o + I(r^{*e} + \dot{s}^e, Z^e) \quad (C.1)$$
$$(ZZ^*) \quad Z^* = G^*_o + C^*_o + I^*(r^{*e}, Z^{*e}) \quad (C.2)$$
$$(PP) \quad P = P(EP^*, \varsigma(Z/K_{-1}, W_o/P^u_o);$$
$$r^{*e} + \dot{s}^e) \quad (C.3)$$

(PP^*) $\quad P^*$ $= P^*(E^*P, \varsigma^*(Z/K^*_{-1},$
$\qquad\qquad W^*_o/P^{*u*}_{o});r^{*e})$ $\qquad\qquad$ (C.4)
(LM') $\quad M'$ $= PL\ (PZ/P)$ $\qquad\qquad\qquad$ (C.5)
$(LM^{*'})$ $\quad M^{*'}$ $= P^*L^*\ (P^*Z^*/P^*)$ $\qquad\qquad$ (C.6)

where: ς = nominal marginal cost at home
$\qquad s$ = log of the real (adjusted) exchange rate
$\qquad\ $ = log $EP^*/P = x + p^* - p$
$\qquad s^*$ = log of real (adjusted) value of home currency
$\qquad\ $ = log $E^*P/P^* = x^* + p - p^*$
$\qquad \dot{s}^e$ = expected rate of real depreciation at home
$\qquad\ $ = $\dot{x}^e + \dot{p}^{*e} - \dot{p}^e$.

Of course the law of one price does not survive the introduction of customer markets for both goods, except as a long-run tendency. Consequently the real adjusted exchange rate, the antilog of s, is no longer equal to one. The prospect of a real appreciation of the foreign currency is therefore possible. The expected real interest rate at home will be higher (lower) than the expected foreign rate by the amount of the expected rate of real appreciation (depreciation) abroad. This relation is used in writing equation (C.1).

The response of this economy to foreign shocks is analysed with the help of figure 4.1, panel A, which has limited similarity to figure 3.1, panel A. Since national demands are entirely funneled to domestic firms, becoming domestic demands, the demand schedules ZZ and ZZ^* in panel A specify national output (not just expenditure) as much as LM' and $LM^{*'}$. Equilibrium corresponds to a pair of intersections occurring at the same r^{*e}. The equations for the right-hand pair of curves in panel A are[4]:

$$(ZZ) \quad Z = G_o + C_o + I\,(r^{*e} + \dot{s}^e, Z^e)$$
$$(LM') \quad M' = \varsigma(Z/K_{-1}, W_o/P^u{}_o)$$
$$\Psi(s;\, r^{*e} + \dot{s}^e)\, L\,(Z)$$

where $\Psi(.)$ is the ratio of price to marginal cost.

The curves in the left-hand frame of panel A are analogous. For expository reasons we first exclude the direct effect of r^{*e} on mark-ups, so LM' and $LM^{*'}$ are treated as vertical, and we take $\dot{s}^e$ to be invariant.

Consider a package of monetary tightening and fiscal stimulus abroad the impact of which is to shift $LM^{*'}$ inward and to shift ZZ^* outward or at any rate not inward. (That ZZ^* does not actually shift in signifies that fiscal stimulus has been injected and has offset the chilling effect that tighter money alone would have on Z^{e*}.) By construction, then, these impacts drive up r^{*e} and drive down Z^*, given s and the expectational parameter $\dot{s}^e$, from the perspective of the left-hand frame. In the right-hand frame there is no impact, given s and $\dot{s}^e$, upon the curves there so the right-hand intersection is unchanged. It follows that the real exchange rate must increase, given the expectational parameter, to reconcile the two intersections. A rise of s will shift $LM^{*'}$ out, pushing back down the intersection there, and shift inward LM', pulling up the intersection there. This real depreciation must proceed until the intersections are in line.

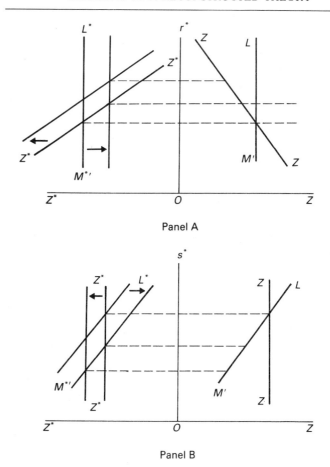

Panel A

Panel B

FIGURE 4.1   An aggregative customer-market model

Therefore *output* in the *home* country is *contracted* in the process. Further, the real interest rate is up and hence home investment expenditure is contracted.

Panel B of figure 4.1 is based on the same two pairs **of equations underlying panel A. In the left-hand**

[61]

frame of panel A the package of foreign policy shocks shifts ZZ^* outward and $LM^{*\prime}$ inward, which implies a fall of s^*. There is no impact on the curves in the right-hand frame. To reconcile the two intersections we require a *rise* of r^{*e}. That will pull ZZ and ZZ^* inward, thus serving to bring the intersections back into line. (The implication that ZZ is pulled in proves that Z must contract.)

A brief remark on these results may be needed here. Doesn't every fool know – even the *jeder esel* of Brahms-Solow lore – that higher interest rates in the USA depress output in Europe? Readers who do not recognize the radical nature of the result here must go back to the previous chapter to study again the message of the orthodox theory: that the rise of interest rates spurs the fixed quantity of European money to achieve faster velocity and thus push up output, and that the sole effects of the reduced investment expenditure are to increase the amount of output that must be exported at a given rate of interest and, since Europe is large, to dampen the worldwide rise of the interest rate resulting from the foreign disturbance, but never to reverse that rise. A novel feature of customer markets is central to the new result: A real depreciation of the European currencies is shown by panel A to drive up European mark-ups, thus curbing the supply of real balances and reducing output in Europe, and to reduce mark-ups in the USA, thus boosting real balances there, until the two interest rates are brought into line again. Figure 4.1's panel B shows that the inward shift of ZZ (which would be negatively sloped in a less extreme case!)

[62]

bites into output only because LM' there has a positive slope to it, owing to the customer-market pricing function, unlike LL in panel B of the earlier figure 3.1.

We want now to bring into the picture the direct effect of the expected real interest rate on the two mark-ups through the respective price-setting functions, an effect suppressed until now, and to discuss the implications of the consolidated analysis for relative functional shares. Since an increase of the interest rate induces firms to widen their mark-ups real cash balances are thereby decreased. Hence the curve LM' in panel A is actually negatively sloped; however we shall suppose it remains steeper than ZZ. Likewise, $LM^{*'}$ slopes "backward" (the wrong way, that is) but, we suppose, not as sharply as ZZ^*. Then, the currency depreciation required by the foreign shocks, in shifting inward the LM' curve in panel A has greater leverage on Z and r^{*e} than when LM' is treated as vertical. In addition, the foreign shocks likewise create a larger disparity of interest rates needing correction by currency depreciation.

There is another consequence of bringing the interest rate into the mark-up functions. Without it the mark-up is implied to widen at home. As a result the share of income at home going to wages is implied to shrink, provided that output per unit of labor is not reduced sufficiently (if at all) by the decline of home output to offset completely the effect of the higher price–wage ratio, which we assume to be the case. In contrast, the mark-up is implied to narrow abroad. Hence the wage share abroad is implied to increase –

doubly so if output slumps abroad as well, and output per unit labor slumps with it, moving procyclically. But our stylized facts record a *fall* of labor's share in the USA in the slump period 1982–85 relative to the previous years, albeit a modest fall, alongside a notable fall of labor's share in Europe at the same time, as predicted by our theory.

It may be, we reason, that some other factor is operating to depress the wage share in *both* areas, making the wage share in Europe fall by a remarkable amount and causing the wage share in the USA to fall on balance. In the customer-market model, the rise of the expected rate of interest plays just that role. Taken alone it pushes down the relative share going to labor in both countries. At the very least the operation of this factor through the mark-up serves to explain – whether or not it uniquely explains – the anomalous fall of the wage share in the USA alongside the unprecedentedly sharp fall in Europe. However, a fuller discussion awaits the section below on supply effects, or the genuine supply effects, of higher real interest rates.

There remains the loose end, the expected rate of future real depreciation of the home currency – equivalently, the future real appreciation of the foreign currency. This expectational parameter is more like a loose cannon on the deck, threatening to make all results unpredictable, unless it can be tied down somehow. To tie it down let us suppose that when the package of foreign shocks occurs, the "virtual" emergence of the real appreciation of the foregn currency that would result, absent a deviation of the expected rate of foreign currency appreciation from its normal value of zero, generates the expectation of a part-way reversion to the normal by the real exchange rate next period; hence $\dot{s}^e$ turns negative.[5] It may be seen that an *increase* (contrary to the reduction just specified) would shift down the ZZ curve in panel A of figure 4.1; the same *foreign* real interest rate would correspond to an increased *home* real interest rate, since lenders could look forward to real currency gains abroad, so that the investment function and ZZ would both shift down when considered as a function of the *foreign* rate. Hence, we see that a *decrease* of the expected rate of real appreciation abroad (as specified) – from zero to something negative – shifts ZZ up. Such a shift, taken alone, requires a real appreciation of the home currency, as it implies a rise of r^{*e} in the right-hand figure while not in the left. But this shift can only moderate the real depreciation of the home currency and the consequent fall of home output that was produced by the foreign shocks according to our previous analysis, since the new expectation of the partial return of the real value of the foreign currency back to its normal level is founded upon the temporariness of its *rise* this period, based on an understanding by the actors in the model that the tight money (which is an element of the package of shocks) has a temporary effect on real interest rates and real exchange rates rather than an undiminishing effect. Thus it does not appear that the expectation of the real depreciation of the foreign currency over the future, when so based is a threat to our previous results.

[65]

4.2 Capital Mechanisms in the Transmission of Real Interest Shocks

In business cycle commentary there has often surfaced the conjecture that slumps typically bring self-destructive as well as self-correcting elements into play. The decline of various investments, that is induced by the slump, operates to lower the nominal demand price, or money wage offered, for a given amount of labor (equivalently, to raise nominal costs more than the demand price for output at a given level of employment and of nominal wage rates). If money wage rates do not resolve the resulting problem by promptly falling to re-equilibrate the labor market (restoring unemployment to its normal, perhaps natural, level) and if demand management by the central bank *et alia* does not or cannot accommodate the disturbance, the result will be increased unemployment. In fact, this view has to negotiate tricky waters to reach port. The reduction of output at given employment acts in the opposite direction to raise wages by raising the market-clearing price level (given a strict monetarist or, *a fortiori*, a liberal monetarist policy). Further, in a closed economy, any decline of capital tends to pull up the profitability of investment, thus stimulating interest rates and the velocity of money. (Hence some theorists list capital among the self-healing elements.[6])

If we were to conceive of Europe and the USA as the whole world, examination of the "world" aggregate data would show that in the 1980s this world has suffered a serious decline of investment, cumulating in a kind of capital-stock shock, brought on by the steep rise of the world real rate of interest. But we would have to admit that the effect upon world employment of this shock could go either way. Its contributory role in the rise of world unemployment and hence European unemployment would be only a theoretical possibility.

We take up for analysis, however, a scenario that is significantly different and more descriptive of the recent period. The monetary disturbance and the personal-income tax reductions in the USA would have produced a worldwide shrinkage of capital, with the world capital market left to work out the distribution of the reductions in capital in each country – indeed there was a decline of investment expenditures in all countries for a time – were it not for the intervention of fiscal investment incentives that served (in the end) to restore US investment to its trend level. Thus the decline of national saving in the USA (plus whatever decline took place in Europe as the result of the transmission of the US shocks) dictated a fall of investment and consequent shrinkage of the capital stock exclusively in Europe.[7]

For a model that generates this scenario we may attach a new subsystem of capital-stock equations to the orthodox aggregative model. Some comments on the interaction of the capital-stock scenario (and our analysis of the other effects of the real-interest rate shock) with the previous customer-market model are reserved for the end of this section.

To describe the effects of the contraction in the

European capital stock we advance in time to the next period – the second period since the onset of the shocks from abroad. There the predetermined beginning-of-period capital stock is K_o, not K_{-1}; the current-period price level is P_{+1} and the expected level of employment next period is $N_{+1}{}^e$. But we shall use the abbreviations K for K_o, P_+ for P_{+1}, $N_+{}^e$ and similarly for the other variables. By way of interpretation we would suggest thinking of the second period as starting with the year 1985; one wants the first period to be long enough to make a difference to K but ideally not so long that the second period has not yet arrived or made its way into the data set.

Because we are studying capital-stock effects on employment we have to write the model so as to make explicit the impact of capital in every equation in which it occurs. The capital-augmented model is

(WAD) $F(K, N_+) + F(K^*, N^*{}_+) -$
$(G_{o+} + C_{o+} + G^*{}_{o+} + C^*{}_{o+})$
$+ (1-d)K + (1-d^*)K^* =$
$K(r^e{}_+, N^e{}_+) + K^*(r^e{}_+ N^e{}_+)$ (K.1)

(LOP) $P^*{}_+ = E^*{}_+ P_+ \ (= E_+{}^{-1} P_+)$ (K.2)

(SS) $F_N(K, N_+) = W_+/P_+,$
$W_+/W_o = (P_+/P_o)^u$ (K.3)

(SS^*) $F^*{}_N(K^*, N^*{}_+) = W^*{}_+/P^*{}_+,$
$W^*{}_+/W^*{}_o = (P^*{}_+/P^*{}_o)^{u^*}$ (K.4)

(LM') $M' = P_+ L(F(K, N_+))$ (K.5)

$(LM^{*\prime})$ $M^{*\prime} = P^*{}_+ L^*(F^*(K^*, N^*{}_+))$ (K.6)

(SFA) $b^* = F_K(K, N_{+1})$
$- F_K(K^*, N^*{}_{+1})$ (K.7)

(KSR) $K^* = K^*{}_{-1}$ (K.8)

[68]

$$(HD) \quad K = K_o < K_{-1} \qquad (K.9)$$

where: N = employment level at home
  K = capital stock at home
  b = subsidy to home investment (expressed as subtraction from interest rate)
  d = proportion of home capital stock lost each period (depreciation) and where the same symbols with the asterisk denote the corresponding variables and parameters abroad.

The first six equations are unchanged from the previous orthodox model, save for making capital and employment explicit, and presumably need no commentary. Equation (K.7) describes the allocation of capital between the two regions. The supposition here is that investors actually achieve *ex post* the equalization of the after-tax or after-subsidy rates of return that they sought *ex ante*. They hit upon the surprise-free allocation. (Of course the very strong hypothesis of rational expectations would imply this equilibrium result.) Equation (K.8) means that the foreign subsidy, b^*, was just enough to result in maintenance of the foreign capital stock at its previous level. The last equation records the effect of the world dissaving in the previous period upon the quantity of capital allocated to the home country. The appended three-equation subsystem adds K, K^*, and b^* to the list of unknowns.

Figure 4.2 compares the no-subsidy scenario, where the capital stock in both countries falls, to the foreign

[69]

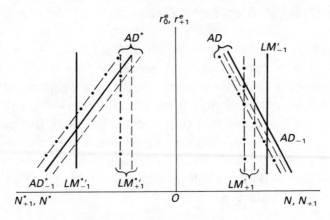

FIGURE 4.2 Capital stock shocks in the augmented orthodox model

investment subsidy scenario that preserves exactly the foreign capital stock. The dashed curves refer to the no-subsidy case, the dash–dot–dash curves to the subsidy case, and solid curves apply to both cases. The two shocks common to the two cases are the foreign tight money, represented by the inward shift of $LM^{*'}$, and the boost of C^*_0 through a cut of personal-income taxation, which taken alone tends to lift AD^*.

In the first period, according to the augmented orthodox model, the effects upon employment are unambiguous, thanks to the liberal monetarist policy, which makes the LM curves vertical. Employment falls abroad but holds up at home, since LM is not at first disturbed by the foreign shocks. The behavior of the AD and AD^* curves in the two cases, subsidy and no-subsidy, is relevant only for the effects on capital in the second period. We specify that in the *no-subsidy*

[70]

case both AD and AD^* may fall a little in anticipation of the negative employment effect next period that reduced capital stocks may have, though not fall so much as to prevent a rise of the real interest rate (on which the fall of investment at home depends). This means that the boost to foreign consumption is only enough to offset the downward shift of AD^* induced by the reduced foreign employment prospect next period directly caused by the continuing tight money. In the *subsidy* case there is again a possible fall of AD, but AD^* unambiguously shifts up, since the investment subsidy increases the interest rate foreign investors can pay. The world real rate is driven higher in this case and world investment, which is unchanged *in toto*, is redistributed toward the foreign country.

In the second period, under the *no-subsidy* scenario, both countries feel the after-shock effects of the decline in the capital stock. Trivially, both regions consequently suffer a decline of output and real income. This follows immediately from equations (K.5) and (K.6) since nominal wage rates never fall, in the model here, in the absence of a fall of the price level, so that a reduced capital stock must drive up the price level at every level of employment. Further, no matter how AD and AD^* behave in the second period, employment will fall in the two countries if and only if the *LM* curves shift inward with a decline of the capital stock. In the *subsidy* scenario, equally clearly, employment and output in the foreign country remain where they were in the first period since the foreign capital stock is exactly preserved by the suitably chosen subsidy, and there is no other

[71]

"dynamic" around; wages, for example, have no life of their own here. The added disinvestment suffered by the home country intensifies the fall of home output and intensifies the fall of employment *if* indeed reduced capital operates to reduce employment by shifting inward the *LM* curve.

The decisive question for the employment effect of the capital-stock shock in the home country is therefore whether, at the initial level of employment, a decline of capital raises the price level via its effect on marginal cost by *more* in proportionate (or percentage) terms than it reduces the demand for real cash balances via its effects on output. A useful starting point, or reference point, is this: if a given decline of capital reduces the marginal product of labor, F_N, by 1 percent, say, thus raising the price level by that percentage amount, and if it reduces the total and hence the average product of labor, F/N, also by 1 percent perchance, and the income elasticity of demand for money is about one, so that the demand for real balances is also reduced by 1 percent, then both the demand and supply of real balances fall equally; by implication, no change of employment is necessary to keep equation (K.5) satisfied. But all the econometric analysis in recent decades suggests that this reference case is quite unrealistic and that, in fact, employment will be contracted by the decrease of the capital stock:

1   Researches into production functions have persuaded most investigators that a decline in the supply of a factor of production tends to raise

[72]

the relative share of that factor in total income. The elasticity of substitution has been widely estimated to be smaller than one. Hence a 1 percent fall in the total and average product of labor, as a result of the decline of the capital stock, would be accompanied by a more-than-1 percent increase in the marginal cost of output. Other things unchanged, the implication is a fall of employment – until the gap between the real supply and real demand for money has been closed.

2   Many econometric analyses confirm that there are slow-moving as well as current elements in the demand for money. Hence a fall of capital and output that was believed by the public to be temporary to some degree (or with some probability) would not occasion as large a reduction in the demand for money as it would if it were believed to be permanent. In contrast, firms are relatively quick to pass on higher unit and marginal costs in the form of higher prices. Other things equal, then, there is a tendency for employment to be contracted in the near term by the capital stock.

3   The reference case above describes an economy in which nominal wages are predetermined or else substantially sluggish within the period. But our model invokes elements of contract theory to deal with the notorious immobility that marks the European labor market, and Edgeworth-optimal contracts almost certainly tie wages with some positive elasticity – which is u in our

[73]

notation – to the consumer price level. Hence the rise of marginal cost and price generated by a fall of the capital stock would trigger a rise of "indexed wages", which would raise the price level some more, and so forth. Our model requires us to weigh the percentage changes of

$$[W_o P_o^{-u}/F_N(K,N)]^{1/1-u} \text{ and } L(F(K,N))$$

as can be seen by solving for P in equation (K.5). If u is near to one, a 1 percent fall of F_N would cause a tremendous percentage increase of marginal cost and price, making a fall of employment certain. (Clearly, if u were equal to one, employment would have to fall proportionately with capital.)

The supply shock mechanism operating through the capital stock can be considered emblematic of a polymorphous collection of real interest effects upon employment applicable to Europe in the 1980s. There are effects of the real interest rate upon the use and maintenance of existing capital, for example. An increase of the real interest rate encourages firms to utilize capital more intensively in the present since the loss of value in the future is now more heavily discounted. This effect, by itself, tends to increase the supply of output in the present, and may tend to increase employment as well (as the analysis in the previous paragraphs suggests), although the cumulative effect is to decrease capital and thus to have the standard supply-shock effects upon output and employment, which we have just reviewed. Another effect works differently: an increase of the real interest rate encourages deferred maintenance. That effect, taken alone, begins immediately to erode the supply of output, and thus (as the above analysis argues) to shrink the demand for labor.

The extraordinary run-up of real interest rates in the 1980s has also produced an effect that ordinarily deserves little attention, the effect on firms' labor hoarding.[8] The holding by firms of a precautionary reserve of employees, a practice called labor hoarding, in part results from a calculation of present costs and *future* discounted benefits. The central administration of a firm subsidizes the hiring of labor by the production department so that in the event of "high" expected demand the desired employee level will then be more nearly available; in the "low" expected demand state the extra labor on hand can "fetch the beer," as D. H. Robertson imagined (in a somewhat different context). If the real interest rate rises during low expected demand, the firm will cut back the implicit subsidy to hiring and training employees, with the result that the production department will allow the workforce to decline from attrition or perhaps from dismissals, the employment contract permitting. The argument rests on the adjustment-cost hypothesis of either rising marginal recruitment or training cost; the precautionary value of having employees is actually inessential. On this cost hypothesis there is a wedge between marginal product and wage, created by the adjustment costs if either the expected discount factor (i.e. $(1+r)^{-1}$) or the expected life-span of employees is finite.[9] In more formal terms, made familiar by models of the adjustment costs of investment in tangible (non-human) capital, if p_I is the minimum possible investment cost of training an employee, λ the shadow worth of a successful training completion, and $1-y_I$ the fraction of that marginal worth offset by the marginal adjustment cost of recruiting and training at some rapid rate I, then

$$p_I + (1-y_I)\,\lambda = \lambda$$

implicitly determines the pace of recruitment and training, given the shadow worth of a success. When the expected real interest rate is increased, λ drops and hence $1-y_I$ (which is an increasing function of I) and thus I must be reduced to re-equate marginal cost to marginal benefit.[10] The macroeconomic consequences of the reduced "subsidy" are a joint contraction of output and employment, precisely like the result of the introduction of a payroll tax on labor. There is no ambiguity regarding the employment effect whatsoever, it may be noted, since there is no second factor of production, such as capital, that is reduced independently of whether or not employment falls.

Another real interest effect we may mention concerns the cash flow of firms and its contribution to productivity.[11] When the real interest rate is increased, there results a decrease in the net cash flow – the flow after deducting the interest payments on bank loans and other short-term instruments – of firms having little or no access to the long-term capital market. It can be argued, however, that it is precisely at those firms whose credit needs would make excessive "information-intensive" demands on the

[76]

creditors, and which cannot therefore find financing in the open auction-type credit market, that the productivity (average and marginal) of labor is the highest; they cannot make the lavish use of capital and labor that the other firms can for lack of full financing. The credit rationing phenomenon thus keeps these firms closer to the shut-down level of operations than the other firms are. Consequently, when the real interest rate rises there tends to be a disproportionate closing of the firms which suffer from credit rationing, which are on the whole more productive than the others. These are not "economic," textbook shut-down since they would be averted if real wages dropped to the lower level consonant with the increased real interest rate, as given by the technological factor–price–frontier relation. Moreover, even when a firm is not forced to close, there may nevertheless be a decline of productivity within the firm as a result of the greater precariousness of its financial situation. These productivity shocks resemble a capital stock shock. The macroeconomic implication is a fall of output and a possible fall of employment.

We note again in closing this section that some of the real-interest effects upon output are slow-working. These in particular can be viewed as contracting output in the "second period" more noticeably than in the first. A corollary effect of that is a rise in the foreign exchange value of the home country's currency – here, a European appreciation. Thus, some of these real-interest impacts (such as the capital stock shock) operate to turn the European currencies around in the second period, producing a movement of exchange

[77]

rates in the direction of recovery. In fact, as is well known, the dollar has been in a declining phase since early 1985, which accord with the implication just noted.

4.3 Real Investment-good Prices in the Transmission of Shocks

The analysis of the transmission of external demand shocks in this section grows out of an old idea that, in application to a closed economy at any rate, has proved too problematic to win acceptance. The proposition is that there exist models in which a contraction of demand depresses the prices of capital goods, not consumer goods, while implicit or explicit employee contracts permit nominal wages to fall (in the neighborhood of the normal employment level) if and only if consumer prices fall, not capital goods prices; hence nominal wages and the general price level are locked together, thus unable to generate the real balance effects needed for the maintenance (or early restoration) of normal employment levels.

The problem with such a theory is that we normally suppose that prices weaken, independently of wages, in the consumer industries when aggregate demand and output fall, and in fact there continues to be some evidence of such price flexibility (perfect or imperfect). An escape route lies in postulating constant short-run marginal costs in the consumer-goods sector, of course, in which case consumer prices may fail to fall with consumer-good output.[12] Another escape

[78]

route is to suppose that consumer demand is invariant to the vicissitudes of current income or, as we have supposed in the present study, that in the "welfare state" the government replaces income lost in the slump with unemployment compensation, relief payments and tax cuts so that aggregate consumption demand does not fall, and neither therefore do consumer prices. But it is not obvious whether these routes are open if the model-builder grants that some (or all) capital goods can shift from the capital-goods industries, where idle capacity has arisen, to the consumer-goods sector; then reduced costs pull consumer goods prices down, initiating a drop of money wage rates and working toward restoration of normal employment.

We find, however, that the contract-theoretic notion of a price–wage failure applies rather well to an open economy struck by certain external shocks. Consider in particular a shift abroad toward tighter money accompanied by a tax cut to hold foreign consumption demand invariant and a new investment subsidy to hold foreign investment expenditure invariant too. The consequent appreciation of the foreign currency tends to shift demand to the home country, raising home prices and lowering foreign prices (though by less than the fall of the home currency, by the law of one price). But suppose that home wages, through the indexation in contracts, must rise in proportion to the home price of consumer goods; the indexation elasticity u is equal to one, to take an easy case. Then no increase of home output of consumer goods will be forthcoming, so domestic consumer good demand will be restored in the foreign country – given our simplifying supposition that national fiscal policies act to stabilize national consumption expenditure and thus stabilize the world total. Hence the fall of price and output abroad is confined to the investment goods sector, which implies a decline in the relative, or real, price of investment goods abroad. By the law of one price, there must also be a decline of real prices in the tradable investment-goods sector at home. Since the home real wage is a constant, by reason of the home country's unit indexation elasticity, this means a decline also of the ratio of the real price of investment-goods output to the real wage, which is also the ratio of the nominal price to the nominal wage. It follows that investment-goods output and aggregate employment will decline in the home country.[13]

To permit a more rigorous analysis we write down a real-investment-goods-price model. Except for our postulates of an accommodative monetary policy with regard to the interest rate and national tax and welfare policies to stabilize national consumption, it differs as little as possible from the orthodox aggregative model. In particular, we adopt the law of one price, in both production sectors to be precise. The new system contains ten equations to determine four nominal prices, four outputs, the exchange rate and (as an addendum) the real rate of interest.

$$(WC) \quad Z_C + Z^*_C = C_0 + C^*_0 \qquad (RP.1)$$
$$(WI) \quad Z_I + Z^*_I = J(r; \ldots)$$
$$+ J^*(r; \ldots) \qquad (RP.2)$$

(LOPC)	$P_C = EP^*_C$	(RP.3)
(LOPI)	$P_I = EP^*_I$	(RP.4)
(SSC)	$Z_C = Z^C(P_C/W, z_C K_{-1})$,	
	$W/W_o = (P_C/P_{Co})^u$	(RP.5)
(SSI)	$Z_I = Z^I(P_I/W, z_I K_{-1})$,	
	$z_C + z_I = 1$	(RP.6)
(SSC*)	$Z^*_C = Z^{C*}(P^*_C/W^*, z^*_C K^*_{-1})$,	
	$W^*/W^*_o = (P^*_C/P^*_{Co})^{u*}$	(RP.7)
(SSI*)	$Z^*_I = Z^{I*}(P^*_I/W^*, z^*_I K^*_{-1})$,	
	$z^*_C + z^*_I = 1$	(RP.8)
(LM')	$M' = M^d(P_C(Z_C + Z_I P_I/P_C))$	(RP.9)
(LM*')	$M^{*'} = M^{*d}(P^*_C(Z^*_C$	
	$+ Z^*_I P^*_I/P^*_C))$	(RP.10)

where, in addition to previous notation:

Z_C = home country output of the consumer good

Z_I = home-country output of the investment good

P_C = nominal home price of the consumer good

P_I = nominal home price of the investment good

z_C = proportion of the home capital stock pre-allocated to the consumer-good producing sector

z_I = proportion of the home capital stock pre-allocated to the investment-good sector

and the same symbols with an asterisk denote the counterpart variables in the foreign country. We stipulate $0 < u \leq 1$ and $0 \leq u^* < 1$. Since indexation is of the essence here we require u to be positive and permit it to equal one (as in the discussion above). We permit u^* to equal zero and cannot permit it to equal

[81]

one, for in that case wages would instantly erase the contractionary effects abroad of the foreign tight money and indeed render foreign money entirely neutral everywhere in the world, according to the present model. Thus, if the *partial* elasticity of the supply of Z_C with respect to $\dot{P}_C$ is a_C, the *total* elasticity found upon taking into account the indexation effect upon the nominal wage is $a_C(1-u) \geq 0$; the corresponding total elasticity abroad is $a^*_C(1-u^*) > 0$. The other partial elasticities may be denoted a_I and a^*_I respectively. Of course, these elasticities refer to the effects of *ex post* price or wage changes, after investing firms have played another round in the guessing game of choosing where to invest capital. We are free to suppose, if we like, that both sectors display "constant costs" *ex ante*, before the commitment of molten capital to one pot or the other; that is,

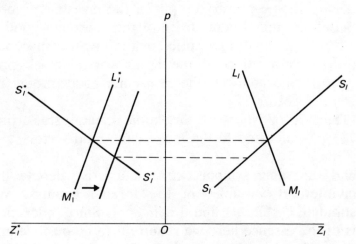

FIGURE 4.3 The real investment-goods price model with tradability

the expectation of a certain small fall of output demanded in a sector would occasion an equiproportionate fall in both the amount of capital invested and the number of employees in that sector, leaving unit costs and the supply price of output unchanged.

Now let us take up again the interesting special case in which the unit indexation elasticity in the home country is equal to one. (The extension to u less than one will be easier to treat as a separate case.) Then the system may be described by figure 4.3. The two supply curves, $S_I S_I$ and its foreign counterpart, have the normal positive slope with respect to the real price of investment goods, although this feature has an unusual basis: supply at home is really a function of P_I/W but since W is proportional to P_C supply is effectively a function simply of the real price, P_I/P_C, which we will denote by p. Abroad, supply is likewise really a function of P^*_I/W^*; but since Z^*_C and therefore P^*_C are undisturbed by the monetary shock, owing to the fixity of the Z_C supply and the fixity of the world consumption demand, W^* is likewise undisturbed, while P^*_I must be proportional to P^*_I/P^*_C, which is p, by the law of one (relative) price. (That is, $P^*_I = E^*P_I = (P^*_C/P_C)P_I = pP^*_C$). The curve $L_I M_I$ and its foreign counterpart appear as surrogate demand curves. They say that, given the consumer-good price, a rise in the relative price of the investment good increases the demand for money at all output levels so that investment-goods output must fall to re-equate the demand for money to the supply. The curve $L_I M_I$ takes P_C and M' as given; the foreign demand curve likewise shifts with a change of the foreign money supply or the foreign consumer price level (which is invariant in the special case under consideration). The equations of the home country curves are

$$(S_I S_I) \quad Z_I = S^I (p, (1-u)P_C; z_I K_{-1})$$
$$(L_I M_I) \quad M' = M^d (P_C(Z_C + pZ_I))$$

and the equations for the foreign curves are analogous. To repeat, we are first focusing on the case $1 - u = 0$ so that P^*_C is a constant.

A tight money shock abroad causes the $L_I M^*_I$ curve to shift inward, which lowers the relative price implied in the left-hand panel. The home country curves are undisturbed. Since Z_C, Z^*_C and P^*_C are invariant to this shock, it is up to E and P_C to reconcile the conflicting intersections in the two panels of the figure. Evidently they must rise enough to shift $L_I M_I$ inward to the point where the relative price p has fallen at home by as much as abroad. Thus the contraction of real cash balances abroad causes a sympathetic contraction of real balances at home, and the consequent world-wide fall of the real price of investment goods results in a decline in the output of capital goods in both countries. Thus employment falls at home as well as abroad.

What is the effect of taking a value of u less than one? Then $S_I S_I$ shifts outward with increased P_C, since at the same p, it now means a higher P_I/P^u_C, hence a higher P_I/W. The effect of this shift is to pull output up while the inward shift of $L_I M_I$ pulls output down. The consequent rise of Z_C raises further complications. It is clear, however, that a high degree of indexation to the consumer price level is sufficient to produce our result: a fall of employment in the home country.

A foreign fiscal shock boosting world demand for the consumer good produces the same crowding out at a distance, or tele-crowding, that was uncovered in the customer-market model. Let us return to the case $u=1$, so that Z_C is fixed, so to speak, by the predetermined home-country real wage, W/P_C. The foreign stimulus to world consumer demand, $C_o + C^*_o$, nevertheless succeeds in raising Z^*_C, since u^* is less than one, and in raising P^*_C. The latter rise means that the same level of $P^*_I//P^*_C$ then corresponds to a higher P^*_I/W^*, since u^* is less than one. In figure 4.3, therefore, $S^*_I S^*_I$ shifts out. The rise of P^*_C and of Z^*_C both clearly shift $L^*_I M^*_I$ in. The effect of these two shifts is to lower p, which implies a contractionary movement down the home country's $S_I S_I$. In order to re-establish intersection with this curve at the new equilibrium point, with lower Z_I and lower p, the price level P_C must rise, given M', to shift $L_I M_I$ to the left by the required amount. Of course, a fall of M' would promote the same outcome, with that much less rise of P_C being required. Either way, we have in this model another demonstration of the "crowding out at a distance" exhibited by the customer-market model. Note that own-country crowding out may share the burden.

A foreign fiscal stimulus to investment demand, by contrast, appears to have no effect on production and employment anywhere, given the model's assumptions of thoroughgoing tradability and liberal monetarism. Since none of the four curves is shifted by this shock, neither Z_I nor the other three variables determined by that reduced subsystem are affected. A subsidy to investment expenditure abroad merely bids up r by increasing the value of J^* at the expense of J. In short, the home country, Europe, simply exports more of its unchanged investment-goods output to the foreign country, the USA. To escape this implication we need to introduce nontradability.

We want now to consider a model in which the investment good is nontradable. Among models without the extreme feature of universal tradability this one seems to be the most convenient, and it is doubtful that having a mixture of tradable and non-tradable investment goods would give significantly different results. To obtain this alternative model we simply replace the world investment equation (RP.2) and the law-of-one-investment-good-price equation (RP.4) with the *national* output-equals-expenditure equations

$$(NI) \quad Z_I = J(r; \ldots) \qquad (RP.2')$$
$$(NI^*) \quad Z^*_I = J(r; \sigma^*, \ldots) \qquad (RP.4')$$

No other equations of the original, tradability model need to be changed. Note that r continues to denote the consumption good rate of interest.

Let us content ourselves with the special case of $u=1$, which represents the extreme case of full indexation in the home country, interpreted again as Europe. Then, as before, W/P_C and Z_C are predetermined constants. Hence Z^*_C and P^*_C/W^* are conditional constants, being increasing functions of the given level of world consumption demand, $C_o + C_o^*$. Nontradability of the investment good, however, leaves p and p^*, the respective real prices of the home-made and foreign-made investment good, not generally equal. Using the home-country investment-good supply curve we substitute the supply price $p(Z_I)$ for p, and using the corresponding foreign supply curve we substitute the supply price $p^*(Z^*_I, (1-u^*)P^*_C)$ for p^*. With these relationships we can reduce the system to the following pair of equations

$$(ZZ) \quad Z_I = J(r; \ldots)$$
$$(LM') \quad M' = M^d(P_C(Z_C + p(Z_I) Z_I))$$

describing the home country and the analogous pair of

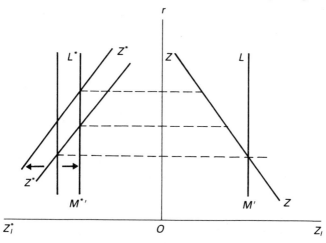

FIGURE 4.4 The real investment-goods price model with non-tradability

[87]

equations describing the foreign country. With these four equations we determine Z_I, Z^*_I, r, and P_C. Figure 4.4 provides the natural diagrammatics.

In this nontradability model a monetary tightening abroad, in shifting $LM^{*\prime}$ inward, drives down p and Z_I, as well as Z^*_I, and drives up r. There is no important difference here from the tradability model. A foreign fiscal stimulus to consumption demand, in lifting Z^*_C and P^*_C, also shifts $LM^{*\prime}$ inward, it may be shown, thus pulling up r again, so that Z_I and p are again pulled down. There is no surprise here either; it is a repetition of the tele-crowding we encountered in the tradability model. The new feature of the present model is that a foreign fiscal stimulus to investment demand, in shifting up the ZZ^* curve, pulls down Z_I and p in the process of pulling up r.

In all these cases the foreign shock drives up the real interest rate forcing a movement up the home country's ZZ curve, which is a contractionary movement. This movement necessitates a rise of P_C – alternatively, a reduction of M' – in order to shift inward the LM' curve by the amount required to bring about a new intersection at the higher equilibrium. The contrast with the orthodox model is now brought into focus. The orthodox model views the rise of the real interest rate as resulting in an upward movement along the LM' curve, and this *expansionary* movement is effected through an upward shift of the other curve via a real currency depreciation. Our supply-price-focused theory views the rise of the real interest rate as resulting in an upward movement along the ZZ curve of figure 4.4 and the similar ZZ curve label in panel A of figure 4.1. This *contractionary* movement is realized through a rise of the consumer price level – or the general price level in the case of the customer-market model – in so far as the home money supply is not contracted in order to prevent that rise of the price level. It is significant that the boost to velocity from the rise of the real interest rate can be accommodated in our figure 4.4 simply by converting our LM' curve to a positively sloped curve like the textbook LM curve. Yet this accommodation does not upset our conclusion that, under full indexation at any rate, there is necessarily a movement up the ZZ curve, hence an induced shift of the sloping LM curve, and thereby a contraction of employment and production in the home country. The orthodox prediction of increased output at home following from the foreign shocks we have specified *cannot* overcome our unorthodox channels under full or near-full indexation. The various demand-price effects of the orthodox theory have a *chance* of predominating if indexation is nil or almost nil.

4.4 The Persistence of the Slump in Europe: Our Supply-price View

Thus far we have only explained how the US shocks could have produced a contractionary disturbance of output and employment in Europe. We must also address the question of why, if the fall of employment in Europe in the early 1980s was indeed generated in this fashion, the disturbance was not followed by

[89]

steady recovery. The economist applying neoclassical theory to the matter will have in mind the concept of the aggregate market labor supply curve which may be locally vertical or backward-bending or positively sloped everywhere. If it is assumed that, in any case, this curve is quite steep in the relevant neighborhood, since career and livelihood are not marginalia for most of us, the neoclassical prediction is that employment will be largely restored, with the requisite reduction of the real wage, once macroeconomic equilibrium is restored. The same prediction is found in the New Classical macroeconomics, provided the participants in the market are persuaded that the shocks are there to stay. The micro–macro models of the past 20 years adduce two reasons for modifying this prediction. If full recovery entails a significant reallocation of labor, the costliness of search will prevent the economy from snapping to its new post-shock position of rest. If full recovery entails a reduction of the general level of nominal wage rates, the nonsynchronousness of wage-rate re-setting by the economy's firms will likewise drag out the process of recovery. But the fact that the unemployment rate in Europe did not even begin to improve, at least in the four major economies there, over the five years 1981–85, points to the need for new explanatory elements to account for this remarkable persistence of the European slump. In fact we have already contributed one such element in pointing to the decline – a decline relative to trend if not an absolute decline – of the European capital stock set in motion by the disturbance of the US shocks to the real rate of interest. Now it is not clear that this process would account for all or a large part of the persistence (let alone the worsening) of the high European unemployment if its sole *modus operandi* were the neoclassical mechanism of a movement down the labor supply curve. However, our essentially contractual view of the European labor market provides very naturally a powerful explanation of strong (though not perfect) persistence.

Our interpretation of the persistence of the high unemployment that arose in Europe in the early 1980s is based on our hypothesis of a considerable degree of real wage stickiness, implemented by private under-standings between firm and employee or enforced by public indexation provisions. If, to take the extreme case, the employee's real wage (in terms of consumer goods) is a constant and if the real cost saving (also expressed in consumer goods) of laying off the employee, which is the true cost of using the employee in production in view of the benefits paid to the laid off, is likewise a constant, in the sense of having been earlier predetermined for the course of his employ-ment, then a decline in the real marginal-revenue productivity of labor as a result of developments such as a rise of mark-ups, a real depreciation of the currency, a fall of the real price of capital goods output, or a contraction of the capital stock, will cause some employees to be laid off. Further, unless the real marginal-revenue productivity schedule is restored, the laid-off members will remain laid off for the balance of their years as employees. In this case of extreme real wage stickiness, it is only the entrance of new workers, in so far as they can make deals for

[91]

employment at reduced real wages in keeping with the reduced real marginal-revenue productivity, that will produce a gradual erosion of the average real wage and a gradual recovery of employment to its normal level.[14] Of course, this vision has all the sharp features of a simple model. In reality, entrants to the labor force subsequent to the shock do not escape the incidence of unemployment. To the extent that customer markets inhibit the rise of new firms to absorb the young while contracts protect laid-off employees from being passed over in favor of cheaper new hires, the new entrants to the labor force will bear a share of the economy's unemployment; indeed, recent entrants will be found bearing an increasing share as the post-shock years accumulate and the laid-off take the place of retiring laid-on. In addition the young have an incentive to wait for better prospects rather than hurl themselves inelastically into contracts for reduced lifetime rewards in immobilizing positions.

The equilibrium unemployment rate – if equilibrium means a correct-expectations, or surprise-free, scenario – is thus increased. The natural unemployment rate – if by that term we mean the equilibrium rate when it is approximately or exactly invariant to (actual and expected) inflation – is thus also increased. Their "long-run" values are not implied to have increased, though. Neither is it implied that the actual unemployment rate always tracks exactly or closely its equilibrium path, as if demand disturbances and erroneous forecasts never happen. It may be especially important to recognize also that, just as economic policy shocks abroad can alter the equilibrium and natural unemployment rate at home, so domestic policy shocks can alter that unemployment rate as well – not *all* shocks, of course, but some. (The question of what Europe can do to help its recovery is the subject of our final pages in this volume.)

This extreme view of labour markets in Europe is oversimplified, we grant. No doubt, the employee's real wage does not hew with precision to a course predetermined upon joining the firm. Thus, the average real wage does not always move sluggishly; it appears to jump a bit. Relatedly, formal wage arrangements in Europe do not provide full indexation; only a varying degree of indexation. For that matter there is not yet a rigorous theoretical defense of full indexation in the optimal contract literature, nor a defense of some kind of generalized indexation (that indexes the wage to the price level and the general wage level, say) that is macroeconomically similar or equivalent to full indexation to the price level.

Nevertheless, the vision of highly indexed (whether or not fully indexed) wage arrangements does generate the phenomenon of persistence. It generates a recovery process of glacial slowness. That is almost good enough for our purposes. What we want, however, is to be able to explain a tendency for unemployment to fluctuate without a clear sign of recovery and even steadily to worsen 2 or 3 years after the shocks have first struck. To do that we need only appeal to the interaction of the contractual vision and the slowdown of the capital stock. As the demographics of young entrants and retirements discussed

[93]

above are operating to bring about a slow recovery of employment, the slowdown of the capital stock is operating in the opposite direction to aggravate the decline.

This observation brings us to our final point. A decline of the capital stock will not produce a decline of employment which will produce in turn another decline of the capital stock and so on, in an endless spiral. Rather, the decline of capital will outstrip that of employment until capital touches bottom. At that time there will no longer will be a force countering recovery of employment. Barring fresh shocks, employment and capital will rise strongly together on a route to complete recovery.

Notes

1   One is reminded of Calvin Coolidge's remark that layoffs of workers tend to cause unemployment, an observation of some subtlety for which he was much derided by political writers.

2   P. Krugman, "International aspects of U.S. monetary and fiscal policy", *Economics of Large Government Deficits*, Federal Reserve Bank of Boston, 1984.

3   This is a somewhat loose account. See E. S. Phelps and S. G. Winter, Jr., "Optimal price policy under atomistic competition," in E. S. Phelps and others, *Microeconomic Foundation of Employment and Inflation Theory*, (Norton, 1970). An important paper on the evidence of large mark-ups is R. E. Hall, "The relation between price and marginal cost in U.S. industry," NBER Working Paper No. 1785, January 1986.

4   We have used the linear homogeneity of the price function to write price as equal to marginal cost, ς, multiplied by a

function $\Psi(s; r)$, increasing in s and r, which gives the price-marginal cost ratio. This substitution is used in LM' and LM'^*.

5 In fact the record of forward exchange rates gives evidence that some return of the dollar was forecast.

6 The conflicting forces are analyzed with a closed-economy model, although more with an oil shock than a capital-stock shock in mind, in E. S. Phelps, "Commodity-supply shock and full-employment monetary policy," *Journal of Money, Credit and Banking*, vol. 10, May 1978. The conflicting effects of a capital-stock shock in a small open economy is briefly discussed in E. S. Phelps, "The effectiveness of macropolicies in small open-economy dynamic aggregative models," Temi di Discussione no. 63, Banca d'Italia, May 1986.

7 A more extreme scenario still would be even more convenient: *world* investment was restored by the powerful investment incentives enacted in the USA so that what occurred was a migration, or reallocation, of capital from Europe to the USA. But in the present model subsidies cannot increase world investment; they can only redistribute investment, since LM curves are made vertical by monetary policies.

8 This effect and some others as well are analysed in J.-P. Fitoussi, J. Le Cacheux, F. Lecointe and C. Vasseur: "Taux d'intérêt réel et activité économique," *Observations et diagnostics économiques*, no. 15, April 1986.

9 S. C. Salop, "A model of the natural rate of unemployment," *American Economic Review*, March 1979, vol. 69, no. 1.

10 See F. Hayashi, "Tobin's marginal q and average q: a neoclassical interpretation," *Econometrica*, vol. 50, January 1982.

11 This paragraph is a first stab at the theme.

12 The late Arthur Okun ventured this postulate in his *Prices and Quantities*, although even there the farm-good sector is exempted from it.

[95]

13 As a result of the shrunken volume of capital goods output, firms will find themselves with more profitable investment opportunities at the margin than they would have had absent the foreign tight money. Moreover, the decline in the relative price of capital goods makes them a better bargain than before, which also raises their rate of return. All firms will want the last unit of the reduced volume of capital goods output, therefore. Consequently they will bid up the real interest rate until the world market for output of the capital goods makers once again clears. In the present model, however, the resulting reduction in the amount of money demanded is automatically accommodated by the central banks.

14 See the overlapping-worker model in P.Dehez and J.-P. Fitoussi, "Wage indexation and macroeconomic fluctuations," in W. Beckerman (ed), *Wage Rigidity and Unemployment* (Baltimore: Johns Hopkins Press, 1986).

5

An Examination of Demand-side Explanations

There is, of course, another proposed explanation of the 1980s slump in Europe. This explanation rests on arguments that there have been demand shocks of monetary or fiscal origin acting to contract employment, and that there are certain mechanisms present in Europe that have operated to turn these employment disturbances into a persisting, chronic phenomenon.

We begin our inquiry into this alternative explanation of the slump with an examination of the hypothesis of weakened demand owing to increased fiscal austerity in Europe. Subsequently we address the hypothesis of domestic monetary shocks. We then take up the various mechanisms that have been seen by some as creating chronic unemployment out of the initial disturbances.

5.1 The Fiscal Austerity Hypothesis

One of the leading hypotheses about the source of the 1980s slump in Europe is the argument, based on

Keynesian analysis, that in this decade among the European countries there have been major fiscal shifts predominantly in the direction of increased fiscal austerity, most notably in the FRG and UK, and this tendency toward decreased public expenditure or increased tax revenue has left Europe with a depressed level of aggregate demand for domestic output.

In its analysis of a small country operating in a regime of flexible exchange rates the orthodox Keynesian theory contains some illuminating (even if ultimately unacceptable) implications in this regard. As the Mundell–Fleming model illustrates, a fiscal destimulus in a country too small to affect the world real interest rate – say the UK – generates an incipient reduction of interest rates there until the implied fall of the UK pound has reached the point where net exports (exports net of imports) have increased enough to fill in for the decline of aggregate demand for domestically produced output accounted for by the fiscal cut-back. This "filling in" is the happy side to the doctrine of open-economy "crowding-out." It was a prime source of the support which grew up in the 1960s for a fluctuating exchange rate.

This Keynesian theory allows a non-negligible effect on employment if the fiscal shift, which in the usual case is appropriately measured by the increase in the high-employment budgetary surplus, is large in relation to world saving, as a "large" country is capable of. The resulting increase in world saving, figured at the initial national output levels, reduces (at least a little) the world real interest rate that borrowers, or the marginal borrower at any rate, can afford to pay – to lower, that is, the World *IS* real rate of interest – and thus lower nominal interest rates in every country. The result is lower employment everywhere. The orthodox model of chapter 3 will be recalled.

Yet the fiscal destimulus occurring in the "large" country (or countries) will fail to yield a net contraction of national employment via this world-real-rate mechanism if simultaneously there occurs elsewhere a fiscal *stimulus* pulling *up* the world *IS* real rate as much (or more) as the fiscal destimulus is pulling down. The accepted method of weighing the fiscal stimulus of one country (or set of countries) against the fiscal destimulus of another country (or set of countries) is to compare "dollar for dollar" the

TABLE 5.1   Measures of the structural budget surplus in excess of the 1980 level as a percentage of the high-employment gross domestic product, Europe and the USA, 1981–85[a]

Country	1981	1982	1983	1984	1985
France	−1.0	−1.4	−1.5	−0.7	0.1
FRG	0.1	1.5	2.6	2.6	3.2
Italy	−3.5	−3.5	−1.3	−1.6	−2.5
UK	2.9	4.4	3.1	2.6	3.1
Weighted sum[b]	−0.2	0.5	1.0	1.0	1.4
USA	0.9	−0.4	−1.1	−1.4	−1.8

Source: Organization for Economic Cooperation and Development, *Economic Outlook* (July 1984), table 8, and (May 1986) table 25.
[a] A positive sign indicates a move toward restriction (surplus).
[b] Weighted by the average US dollar value of each country's GDP in 1980 prices.

[99]

decrease in the high-employment budget surplus in the former country to the increase in the high-employment budget surplus in the latter country. Later we shall examine a re-calculation of the changes in these surpluses to allow for inflation adjustments. Here we content ourselves with the conventional measures, which are shown in table 5.1. These estimates suggest that the tendency toward increased surpluses in Europe over the 1980s has been more than offset by the tendency toward a decreased algebraic surplus – a gigantic deficit in fact! – in the USA. Using a similar method Lawrence Summers and Olivier Blanchard reached much the same conclusion for a wider collection of countries that includes Japan: "[W]e found no evidence in favor of the thesis that [budgetary] deficits are leading to low saving: in the OECD as a whole, there has been little change in structural public dissaving . . .".[1]

This method of weighing fiscal stimuli understates the effect of the shift in US fiscal policy that was legislated in late 1981 (and amended in 1982), however. Since the channel by which the European fiscal shifts have contracted European output, according to the orthodox mechanism now under discussion, is the world real interest rate, we must give special weight to those elements of the US fiscal stimulus that exerted a peculiarly powerful upward pull on the real interest rate: the investment tax credit and shortening of the depreciation schedules, which greatly increased the (after-tax) marginal efficiency of investment by US corporations. Indeed, if one were to go to the extreme position represented by the notorious "Treasury view"

[100]

of the 1920s, in which the short-term real interest rate is equal to the marginal productivity of capital, and were to modify this doctrine to allow for investment subsidies, we would have a model in which tax induced consumer spending and ordinary public expenditure, and hence the deficit *per se*, would have no current effect on the short-term real rate of interest, while an investment subsidy would have the classical effect of raising the short-term rate. Financial analysts studying the implications of the US legislation commonly estimated the effect on the after-tax rate of return of the US investment stimuli to be on the order of two percentage points (that is, 200 basis points). Yet this is an underestimate, since it is a base-year-weighted average though the economy will not be constrained to make the base-year mix of investments; instead the investments with the greatest increase in after-tax return will be favored. Hence the effect on the marginal efficiency of investment after tax may easily have been around four percentage points or more. Recent events are providing a further basis for estimation. In 1986 the investment tax credit was suspended, effective retroactively, and more realistic depreciation schedules were legislated to apply in future years. It is presumably not a coincidence, then, that over 1986 and the early part of 1987 (up to this writing) expected real rates of interest have been perceived as drifting to markedly lower levels; some of the recent rise in stock market prices around the world is widely interpreted as constituting corroborative evidence of reduced expectations of the real rate of interest on alternative assets.

[101]

Various extensions and fine points of the orthodox Keynesian theory do nevertheless open the door at least a crack to the possibility that fiscal destimulus in the UK, the FRG, and certain other European countries, is not cancelled by fiscal stimuli outside Europe of equal or, within limits, much greater magnitude. The empirical likelihood of each of these uncancelled effects on employment and the quantitative importance of them are another matter.

1   The national fiscal destimulus in a country (or countries), if it generates expectations of falling public debt and (on balance) rising after-tax national income over the future, may instil projections of increased demands for money in the future and thus lower future prices. The expectation of such deflation or disinflation will operate to lower the nominal interest rates that businesses are willing to pay – the national *IS* nominal interest rate, in other words – thus increasing the quantity of real cash balances demanded in the present and (unless the central bank accommodates) hence reducing output and employment.

2   The national fiscal destimulus, if it causes a (significantly large) relative fall in the demand for the "home good" – the good (or goods) of which the country is the comparatively large producer (compared to the rest of the world) – or if it falls (appreciably) on a non-traded good, may cause a fall in the relative price of that good and thus a real depreciation of the country's

currency. The expectation of an eventual rise back to normal of that relative price operates to lower the real rate of interest that businesses can pay in terms of the "home good" and more generally the basket of goods produced by the country; equivalently, the prospective fall back to normal of the real exchange rate (that is, the real price of foreign currency) lowers the domestic real rate of interest available to lenders. The resulting fall of the nominal rate of interest increases the quantity of real cash balances demanded and (unless the central bank counters it) thus contracts employment.

3 If the fiscal destimulus leads the central banks of some other countries to lower their interest rates in step with the fall in the interest-rate decline in the country engaging in the destimulus, in order that their currencies depreciate in line with the first country's, the fall of the world real interest rate and of the country's domestic real interest rate may thereby be magnified; less of the "multiplier effect" of the fiscal destimulus is sent abroad, more is bottled up at home. The nominal interest rate and employment are contracted on this account.

In principle, then, the orthodox open-economy theory admits the possibility that the shift toward fiscal austerity that appears to have occurred in Germany, to take the clearest example, could have had a contractionary impact on employment in Germany despite a simultaneous fiscal stimulus abroad that is two, four, or even ten times the size of the destimulus.

Whether in fact such shifts as we infer toward fiscal austerity in certain European countries more than offset the buoyant effect on employment there which orthodox theory says tended to result from the opposing US shift toward fiscal ease is an empirical question on which it is difficult to have a very strong conviction *a priori*. The obvious test is to examine directly the available evidence on the orthodox channel: to look at nominal interest rates. If indeed the FRG shift outweighed the US shift, we should find lower nominal rates in the FRG during the slump – and *a fortiori* so if it is granted that the low employment of the 1980s *per se*, whether or not due in any part to FRG austerity, lowered nominal interest rates by reducing expectations of wage inflation accordingly.

The behavior of nominal interest rates, once examined, must come as a shock to those who by force of habit liken Europe in the 1980s to the slack demand era of the 1930s. As table 5.2 shows, nominal interest rates were higher, not lower, everywhere but Denmark in both 1983 and 1985 than in 1977, and higher in most countries than in 1979. In the FRG, it is true, nominal rates were lower in the two later years than in 1979, but the average of the 1983 and 1985 levels was nevertheless higher than the average of the 1977 and 1979 levels. The pattern in the UK is the same in this respect. The nominal rate average for the two 1980s years exceeded the average for the two earlier years.

Viewed from the perspective of orthdox theory,

[104]

then, it is impossible from nominal interest-rate data to confirm any Keynesian deficiency of aggregate demand in Europe. Although such fiscal austerity as arose in Europe did presumably dampen some of the European countries' *ISXM* curves, the interest rate record does not indicate a significant net decline of those curves; on the contrary, it suggests a net rise in most of the European countries. In other words, while the European fiscal shifts may have had a predominantly negative influence on domestic aggregate demand, reducing $G + C$ in the aggregate demand sum $C + I + G + X - M$, they were not sufficient to outweigh (or perhaps even to offset) the rise of $X - M$ emanating from the opposite fiscal impulses in

TABLE 5.2   Nominal money market rates, Europe and the USA, selected years, 1977–85[a]

Country	1977	1979	1983	1985
Belgium	5.49	7.97	8.18	8.27
Denmark	14.48	12.63	12.03	9.97
France	9.22	9.48	12.63	10.08
FRG	4.37	6.69	5.78	5.44
Italy	14.03	11.86	18.44	15.25
Norway	9.84	8.39	12.27	12.16
Sweden	9.96	8.19	10.85	13.85
UK	8.06	13.59	9.90	11.95
USA	5.54	11.20	9.09	8.10

Source: International Monetary Fund, *International Financial Statistics*, various issues.

[a] Call money rate for all countries except France (Interbank money rate), FRG (Interbank deposit rate), UK (Treasury Bill rate), and USA (Federal Funds rate).

[105]

the USA. (From the point of view of orthodox theory, it might be added, the nominal rate data are consistent with the hypothesis that the US shocks drove up nominal rates in Europe, thus energizing velocity and creating a demand-side fillip to European employment).

If in fact the European shifts toward fiscal austerity did not have contractionary demand-side effects strong enough to outweigh (or even in most cases to offset) the expansionary demand-side effects of the increase of nominal interest rates coming from the US shocks, it remains possible that the fiscal austerity was great enough to prevail through other mechanisms. There may have been contractionary effects on domestic employment via supply-price effects. Our customer-market model and two-sector models have the property that certain kinds of fiscal destimuli in a country, such as the UK or FRG, may leave employment lower on balance, despite a simultaneous demand-side stimulus from foreign disturbances such as the US shocks, without leaving nominal interest rates likewise reduced on balance. To put the matter in the simplest terms: some domestic fiscal destimuli both shift the *ISXM* curve downward *and* shift the *LM* curve inward. Some external fiscal stimuli, such as the US shocks, shift the *ISXM* upward while shifting the *LM* curve inward. Clearly such a destimulus, in contracting employment partly through *LM*, achieves a given contraction either with no tendency to reduce the nominal rate of interest (because *LM* shifts far along a negatively sloped *ISXM* curve) or with comparatively little tendency to reduce the nominal

[106]

rate, compared to a pure *ISXM* destimulus. Thus the effect of the domestic destimulus on *employment* might overcome the external shock's expansionary effect (if indeed that was the case), or might instead reinforce the external shock's contractionary effect, leaving employment unambiguously lower, while its effect on the *interest rate* was either upward, reinforcing the external shock, or too weak in its downward effect to overcome the upward effect of the external shock, thus leaving the interest rate higher. The point is that we cannot weigh the total contractionary effect of the domestic destimulus against the (total) effect of the external shock simply by measuring the net effect on the nominal interest rate, since the destimulus has an *LM* dimension to its effect as well as an *IS* dimension.

Figure 5.1 illustrates the two relevant cases. In

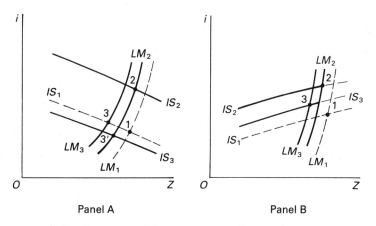

Panel A   Panel B

FIGURE 5.1 Output and interest rate effects of domestic fiscal destimulus (second shock) following a foreign fiscal stimulus (first shock).

panel A the demand effect of the domestic destimulus, in outweighing the demand effect of the foreign stimulus, would yield (via the *ISXM* curve labeled for brevity *IS*) a net decline of the nominal interest rate (to accompany the net decline of employment) if unopposed by supply-price effects. But the supply-price effects of the destimulus and of the foreign stimulus both operate (via *LM*) to reduce employment further while raising the interest rate – enough in the case shown to leave the interest rate higher.

The case shown in panel B differs in two ways: the supply-price effects tend, other things equal, to *lower* the interest rate, but the action in this respect is not great enough to overcome the net tendency of the demand effects to pull the interest rate *up*. Yet, because *LM* curves are steep, the supply-price effects are decisive for employment, both of them ensuring a decline of employment.

There may be a danger that the message here will be misread. We have not argued that fiscal destimulus at home contracts employment while necessarily masking this effect by raising the interest rate at the same time. The argument is that the foreign stimulus raises the interest rate whether increasing or decreasing employment. From this altered position the domestic destimulus may very well contribute to a decline of employment without reversing, or overcoming, the rise of the interest rate.

If the failure of nominal interest rates to fall in the 1980s in most of the European countries is inconclusive evidence that European fiscal austerity over this period has been weak or non-existent – too weak

to have contributed appreciably to the 1980s slump –
we are compelled to rely more heavily on the direct
evidence of the magnitude of the European fiscal
impulses. In table 5.3 we examine anew this evidence,
this time focusing on the inflation-adjusted measures
of the structural budget surplus prepared by the
OECD. Of course, we are all aware of how problematic such inflation adjustments are. It is striking
nevertheless to see that in all but one of the four
major European economies, namely the FRG, the
OECD measure of the inflation-adjusted structural
budgetary surplus is *lower* by 1983 and *remains lower*
through 1985 than in 1980. In the UK, which has
gained a reputation for hard-nosed fiscal soundness,
the structural surplus after inflation adjustment *fell* by
nearly 2 percent of the gross domestic product. This

TABLE 5.3   A measure of the inflation-adjusted/structural budget
surplus in excess of the 1980 level as a percentage of the high-
employment gross domestic product

Country	1981	1982	1983	1984	1985
France	−1.0	−1.4	−1.5	−0.9	−0.3
FRG	0.1	1.6	2.5	2.4	2.9
Italy	−5.0	−5.4	−3.2	−5.3	−6.9
UK	0.5	0.6	−1.9	−2.6	−1.7
Weighted sum[b]	−1.0	−0.6	−0.5	−0.9	−0.6

Source: Organization for Economic Cooperation and Development,
Economic Outlook (July 1984), table 8, and (May 1986), table 25.
[a] A positive sign indicates a move toward restriction (surplus).
[b] Weighted by the average US dollar value of each country's GDP in
1980 prices.

[109]

makes the failure of nominal interest rates there to fall all the more understandable; foreign and domestic fiscal impulses were all pulling them up, and only the expectation of disinflation was pushing them down. In Italy the same adjusted structural surplus fell by nearly 7 percent of the gross domestic product. This accords well with the strong comparative rise of nominal interest rates in Italy, and with the comparative strength of the currency.

It can hardly escape notice that among the four major European economies there does not appear to be the predicted relationship between the (algebraic) increase in the adjusted structural surplus and the increase of the unemployment rate over the same period. Italy is the least bad in the fiscal column but is second-worst in regard to the rise of unemployment, its 5.4 point increase from 1980 to 1985 being second only to the 6.0 point increase in the UK. The FRG ranks the worst in the fiscal colummn while its unemployment rise from 1980 to 1985 was second-best, bettered only by France (which suffered a further rise in 1986, however, so that the FRG may now be best).

These last observations perhaps nail the coffin of the hypothesis that much of the European slump is attributable to increased fiscal austerity. That hypothesis is already dead, as we have just seen; killed by the brute fact that for the four major European countries as a whole there was a *decline* of austerity; and even if this is only a mismeasurement, there is utterly no possibility of a true increase of austerity on a scale large enough to make an appreciable difference. We now find, however, that the Keynesian hypothesis cannot help to explain the differences in the rise of unemployment among the major European countries.

Ought it not to be conceded, in all candor, that these last observations also present an anomaly for our own models? After all, our customer-market model and two-sector models have the property that domestic fiscal destimulus has both an *IS* and a *LM* contractionary effect on employment, do they not? The truth is more complicated. The two-sector model does imply a positive employment effect from the *capital-good* spending by the government, in the large-country case which is the subject there; this positive effectiveness carries-over to the small-country case if (and only if) the capital good or goods purchased by the government are non-tradable. But an increase in purchases of consumer goods by the government or by households in response to an income-tax cut is not implied to have an expansionary effect on employment. The customer-market model does have conventional implications about the effects of government spending in general. But that model does not promise multiplier effects greatly above zero, owing to crowding-out of investment. (The same negligible effectiveness may apply to the US budgetary deficit, of course; it may be that only the subsidies to US investment have appreciable power to disturb the system, thanks to their powerful effect on the real interest rate.) Hence the theoretical framework advocated here is not fundamentally undermined by the finding that intra-European differences in fiscal

[111]

stimulus do not apparently help to explain intra-European differences in unemployment experience in the 1980s.

Before closing our analysis of the Keynesian hypothesis we should take the opportunity to bring in an interesting variant of the Keynesian theme. It has been suggested that the European fiscal impulses are an underestimate of the sag in aggregate demand for they do not include the decline of European consumer demand (at any given level of European output) that must have resulted from the fall of European wealth brought about by the American shocks via the increased real rate of interest.[2] This mechanism could be extended to embrace the rise in the real domestic-goods value of the dollar indebtedness of European governments and private firms and persons. It must be emphasized, however, that if this consumer-demand effect is embedded in the orthodox model laid bare in chapter 3 it can only serve to moderate the worldwide rise of the real rate of interest; it cannot overturn the net stimulus transmitted through the nominal interest rate on to the velocity of money.

5.2 The Tight Money Hypothesis

Europe's own monetary policies may also have played a role in the recent slump. This may be so whether the stock of money was the target of policy or, instead, some sort of interest rate or the exchange rate. What we may call the monetarist hypothesis proposes that a large part of the slump is attributable to "tight money," by which is meant a deceleration of the money supply. In some models, as is well known, a deceleration of the money supply has "effectiveness" in contracting employment if and only if it is unexpected; in some other models featuring non-synchronous price setting or wage setting, a deceleration will have some effectiveness even if expected at the beginning of the current period, and indeed even if anticipated fully over the past. If the observed deceleration of the money supply was unexpected, the main difference between the two classes of models is that synchronization of wage and price setting facilitates the economy's tendency to bounce back after the shock has disturbed things. Note, finally, that in some models the unexpected change of the money supply is a proxy for the unexpected change in the variables of which the money supply is a function; an unexpected shock, in causing an unexpected (incipient or realized) weakening of interest rates or of the currency value in international markets, might be the cause of the unexpected decrease of the money supply.

The record of growth rates of the money supply in the four major European economies are shown in table 5.4 alongside the growth rate of the US money supply, as tabulated by the International Monetary Fund. We see a sharp slowdown of the European money supply in 1980, much more marked than that shown in the US data. In the USA the growth rate subsequently rises to a level higher than before for awhile, thus offsetting the well-known fall of the velocity of money around 1981, which is widely credited to the expectations of disinflation instilled by

TABLE 5.3

	1978	1979	1980	1981	1982	1983	1984	1985
France, FRG, Italy, UK	13.3	12.8	10.1	10.8	10.0	10.1	8.3	9.0
USA	8.5	8.3	8.0	9.4	9.3	12.5	8.0	9.1

the US government at that time. In contrast, the growth rate of the money supplies in Europe remains low, and it takes another drop in 1984.

It does not detract from the thesis of this monograph to grant that the worsening of European unemployment early in the decade – say, in 1981, to be precise – is largely attributable to this sharp slowdown of the European money supply. Had the growth rate of the money supply been maintained, it may be argued, the European currencies would have weakened further (more than they did), and although nominal wage rates would quickly have nullified some substantial part of the real effects (and ultimately would have erased all the effect in so far as money is neutral), some of the actual dip of output and employment in Europe would thereby have been averted.

The crux of the issue over the part played by European monetary policies is whether this one-time deceleration (if we pass our eyes over the smaller repetition 4 years later) is sufficient to account for most (or all) of the behaviour of unemployment over the more than half a decade under study. We shall argue that the monetarist explanation is deficient,

[114]

even if it is credited with causing "aftershocks" through the stock of capital. The monetarist hypothesis suffers from two anomalies, one pertaining to the accompanying behaviour of the inflation rate and one involving the dynamics of the unemployment rate.

The first weakness of the monetarist explanation is that it cannot explain the fact that the average inflation rate among the four major European economies continues unabated until (but not including) 1983. Indeed, as table 5.5 recording the growth rate of the gross domestic product deflator shows, the rise of the price level in 1982 was still noticeably *higher* than in the late 1970s and earlier – and this despite the influence tending to slow down nominal wage growth (and thus price-level growth) that was presumably exerted by the greatly increased unemployment rate then prevailing. In contrast, our explanations, in which the US shocks are portrayed as pushing up the supply price of European output, are well adapted to the harsh facts of undiminished or actually increased inflation in the early 1980s.

The other difficulty faced by the monetarist hypothesis is the timing of the unemployment rise in

TABLE 5.5

	1968–77	1978	1979	1980	1981	1982	1983	1984
France, FRG, Italy, UK	8.2	8.7	9.0	11.1	9.8	9.4	7.2	5.6
USA	6.5	7.3	8.8	9.1	9.6	6.5	3.8	3.9

Europe. The rise of the unemployment rate in 1980 over the previous year is only about a half a percentage point, and the rise in the next year is less than two percentage points. But the unemployment rate rises relentlessly, year after year, until reaching a plateau more than five percentage points above its 1980 level. If the response had been the other way around, with a surge of unemployment followed by gradual improvement, the monetarist explanation would be a great deal more plausible. It is a serious strike against the monetarist hypothesis that the unemployment rate was still rising by one and a half percentage points over the previous year in 1982 and by more than one percentage point as late as 1983, 3 years after the slowdown of the money supply. In a world without indexation such long lags in the response of unemployment to money might be laid with some plausibility to staggered wage and price setting. The argument could be made that the tendency of the unemployment rate to recover was steadily overcome by the *repeated* suppression of the money-supply growth rate, in 1981 and subsequent years, which always came as a disappointment – as bad "news" – to price and wage setters. But the extent and degree of wage indexation in Europe makes staggered wage setting a much weaker reed on which to base such an argument than it would be in the USA, for example. At some point the hypothesis that the public was expecting a much higher money supply than materialized ceases to be able to bear the required load.

There is also the issue of whether the money-supply

[116]

deceleration is necessary. We might go so far as to suggest that the disturbance to the real interest rate in Europe by the shocks abroad caused the demand for money to decline, on balance, primarily by increasing the nominal interest rate (as emphasized by the orthodox theory) and by reducing the real price of the investment-good output (as shown in our two-sector models); and that the money authorities in decelerating the money supply were accommodating that decline in demand, more or less. To that extent they were not engineering an output contraction but, rather, contriving the decrease of liquidity that would otherwise have occurred through a large jump of the price level.

Theorists not ready to abandon demand-oriented theories of the European slump have nevertheless succeeded in producing some novel and interesting explanations of how a decline of demand in Europe, from either Keynesian or monetarist causes, might cause the unemployment rate to remain swollen for a prolonged period, and even to grow worse for a few years after the initial shock. We shall briefly comment on these ideas and compare them to the view that we take here.

5.3 The Hysteresis Effect Required by Demand-side Explanations

To solve the problem that if Europe faced only the demand shocks of 1980 and earlier ones, it would be predicted to have been recovering to its natural rate of unemployment since then, several economists have argued that unemployment behavior in Europe now displays "hysteresis." In the present context this concept implies that a deviation from equilibrium causing abnormally high unemployment last year pulls up the natural unemployment rate this year. (More generally, it pulls up the locus of equilibrium unemployment rates corresponding to alternative expected and actual rates of wage or price inflation.) "In this case, one cannot speak of an *ahistorical* equilibrium locus. . . . The *live* hand of history produces an hysteresis effect: The time path to equilibrium shapes that equilibrium."[3] Evidently such a hysteresis effect is quite different from the persistence phenomenon due to nonsynchronous wage-price setting or to recruitment-search costs, in which unemployment gradually returns to the *same* steady-state equilibrium (or equilibrium locus) which was available before. Three sources of such a hysterisis effect have been proposed as possibly important in explaining the prolonged or worsening effect of the hypothesized demand-side in Europe.[4]

One of these hysteresis mechanisms involves the employability of those who fall victim to unemployment. Young workers who lose their jobs, or who are unable to win them upon entering the workforce, though perhaps earning sporadic wage income in short-term jobs that occasionally arise, miss during their unemployment the opportunity to gain experience and other prerequisites needed to gain admission to a fulfilling career in some steady, or long-term, job.[5] Two effects can result. First, with fewer workers able to signal their qualifications there will be fewer long-term jobs offered and held over the future, even in normal-demand years. Second, deprived of a sense of advancement and belonging, many of these young workers develop emotional disabilities or other personal problems that make it difficult or impossible for them to qualify for long-term employment later. Older workers who lose their jobs encounter the problem that some firms need years to amortize the costs of on-the-job firm-specific training and, moreover, they see older workers as often having less incentive not to quit or shirk. Thus the loss of employment renders some of these older workers semi-unemployable, increasingly so as they grow older. Although these effects are of unquestioned importance with regard to the social costs of unemployment, and have received much study in the context of the Great Depression, there is not even a body of opinion to point to, let alone a consensus, on the magnitude of their impact on the natural rate of unemployment. There has been no suggestion, however, that today's unemployed in Europe have all become unemployable, or even that more than a small minority have yet suffered this effect.

The second mechanism, whether or not a true example of hysteresis, centers on the role of the capital stock. The drop of employment hypothesized to result from demand-side shocks, such as a slowdown of the money supply, triggers a cessation (or at any rate a sharp fall) of investment; the consequent slowdown of the capital stock may very well raise the supply price of output more (holding employment as given) than it raises the demand price for output; such an effect might be large enough to offset or even outweigh for a while the opposing tendency of the slowdown of money wage rates resulting from the reduced level of economic activity to bring a recovery of employment.[6] Thus, in the tug-of-war between capital and wages, it is possible for capital to make unemployment worse before, with the eventual recovery of investment spending, unemployment gets better. But if it is the case, as demand-side explanations assume, that there is little or no indexation of wages to the price level, so that there is no so-called real wage rigidity present to buttress the possibly contractionary effect of the slowdown of the capital stock, then it is quite doubtful that the employment effect of the capital-stock, if indeed contractionary, would be strong enough to offset or outweigh the employment effect of falling money wage rates. Clearly it would be logically impermissible for an advocate of demand-side explanations to pooh-pooh real wage rigidity in Europe, thus weakening supply-price explanations and strengthening demand-side ones, then to re-admit real wage rigidity in order to potentiate the contractionary effect of the capital stock slowdown that is in turn attributed to demand-side shocks.

The third hysteresis mechanism to become widely discussed derives from the insider–outsider theory of employment and wage determination.[7] The key premise is that the insiders – those who were members of the firms' workforce last period – simply set the wage this period at such a level as to expect to remain employed, with utter disregard for the consequences to the outsiders. When a transient demand shock generates a bulge of new unexpected hires this period, the increased workforce at the typical firm constitutes the increased base level of employment next period, which unexpected new hires or dismissals due to a shock next period may add to or subtract from. The enforcement mechanisms here range from organized labor unions to informal protests and harassment. The theory has been strengthened and extended in a number of directions. There are, however, some conceptual questions that need to be answered: How is it that a laid-off employee is denied his former voting rights? And why does the employer promise (absent future shocks) lifetime employment to the newly hired, albeit at a real wage that may be lower than what the initial money wage is expected to be worth in real terms, when the employer and these workers could have reached such a bargain before but revealed an unwillingness to do so? Whatever the answers, there is undoubtedly an element of truth pointed to by the insider–outsider theory. The principal issue is the empirical one of how much persistence in the unemployment rate this theory generates. A recent statistical inquiry into hysteresis hypothesis indicates that wage inflation was noticeably higher in France and the UK in the early 1980s than the fitted wage equation predicts, although the reverse was true of the FRG.[8] That suggests that wage indexation and supply-price shocks are part of the story, a part not captured by persistence. One suspects that *price* equation residuals would be more striking. Finally, it is hard to see how this theory of persistence can explain the conspicuous worsening of the unemployment situation in the 1980s through 1985, especially when, judging by the naked eye, this theory never seemed capable of generating a marked prolongation of slumps in the 1950s and 1960s, let alone the phenomenon of slow worsening. A great deal more econometric work must be done before it can be said that demand-side explanations of the European slump are not in trouble.

In attempting to appraise the importance of demand-side explanations of the 1980s slump in Europe it is natural to examine the unemployment rates found elsewhere in the world. Our supply-price mechanisms clearly imply that the American shocks have operated in the direction of raising unemployment in *all* other countries, not just the European countries. In contrast, demand-side explanations imply that we will find a major slump only in those other countries that, like Europe, have suffered an adverse demand shock. The evidence on this score is certainly favorable to the hypothesis that the US shocks, through the world real rate of interest, have exerted a strong contractionary influence. Most of the other countries of the world, European and non-European alike, had a much larger unemployment rate and larger percentage gap of output from its trend path in 1985 than in 1980. To encompass this rise of unemployment in other continents the advocates of demand-side explanations must argue either that there was a wave of demand shocks around the world which occurred either by coincidence or as a result of the US shocks. Whatever the truth of the matter, this

[122]

evidence of a worldwide slump outside the USA places the burden of proof on demand-side explanations. Our supply-price-based hypotheses make this worldwide slump easily understandable, while it is not yet clear that demand-side explanations can plausibly interpret this striking pattern.

Notes

1 O. J. Blanchard and L. H. Summers, "Perspectives on high world real interest rates," *Brookings Papers on Economic Activity*, 1984:2 (Washington, DC: Brookings Institution), pp. 273–334.
2 J. Frenkel and A. Razin, "Budget deficits and rates of interest in the world economy," *Journal of Political Economy*, June 1986.
3 E. S. Phelps, *Inflation Policy and Unemployment Theory* (London: Macmillan, 1972), pp. 77–78.
4 For a wide-ranging survey (with some original developments) see O. J. Blanchard and L. H. Summers, "Hysteresis and the European unemployment problem," Harvard Institute of Economic Research, Discussion Paper 1240, May 1986 (mimeo), p. 78.
5 "Getting to work on time . . . getting to be 'reliable' and learning to work with other people are necessary for continuation in the job," in Phelps, *Inflation Policy*, p. 79.
6 This possibility is analyzed in E. S. Phelps, "The effectiveness of macropolicies in small open-economy dynamic aggregative models," Banca d'Italia, Temi di Discussione no. 63, May 1986, p. 46.
7 This theory is developed in a series of papers by A. Lindbeck and D. J. Snower. See their "Wage setting, unemployment, and insider–outsider relations," *American Economic Review*, vol. 76 (May 1986) and the references there. The earliest known discussion is R. E. Hall, "Unionism and the inflation-

ary bias of labor markets," Berkeley, Calif., 1970. Some implications are noted in Phelps, *Inflation Policy*, pp. 76–78.

8 Blanchard and Summers, 1986.

6

Can Europe Do It?

In 1929, when unemployment in Britain was already well along on its climb to Great Depression levels, Lloyd George announced his pledge to reduce unemployment to "normal proportions" through a plan of public expenditure on capital goods, if his party won the next general election.[1] Keynes wrote a pamphlet in support of the plan under the title: "Can Lloyd George Do It?"[2] There was increased public spending in Britain, and Britain did emerge comparatively early from the worst depths of the Depression. Whatever the readiness of economists now to credit public spending then with effectiveness in helping Britain out of the 1930s Depression, today there are widespread questions about the effectiveness and costly side-effects of fiscal (and monetary) remedies for Europe's 1980s slump. Commenting on the parallel between then and now, and finding no evidence that fiscal stimulus can be much help, the Viennese economist Michael Wagner declared, "Lloyd George would not make it today either."[3]

Although doubts surround all the conventional anti-unemployment weapons – only socialism is conceded to have sure-fire effectiveness – there seems to be a particularly acute consciousness in Europe of the drawbacks of monetary policy. There is, first, the matter of its effectiveness, costs aside. The impression has grown that the high degree of indexation in Europe has robbed monetary stimulus of a great deal, perhaps most, of its effectiveness. Granted, even in those present-day models of staggered wage and price setting in which monetary policy is considered quite powerful, there being little or no indexation of wage offers (and price offers!) to the general price level (and/or general wage level), a one-time increase of the money supply relative to trend is implied to have only a transient effect on the paths of output and employment. The presence of full or near-full indexation of wages to the price level, however, reduces the half-life of the "transient" rather drastically. Moreover, if so much of the effect soon takes the form of a higher level of prices and wages, the therapeutic value of the injection for the capacity-utilization expectations of firms making investment decisions is that much diminished.

It is true that in most real-life economies, where the domestic real interest rate is not continuously equalized to the world real rate of interest, the domestic real interest rate is a feasible target of monetary policy, at least for a while. Then a country can lower the target real interest rate by central bank means in order to stimulate employment. But suppose that, as a result of supply-price shocks such as we have discussed, the equilibrium and natural unemployment rate is swollen. Then engineering a recovery of employment to "normal proportions" by this method risks reducing the unemployment rate below the swollen natural rate; the result of doing that will be an indefinite inflation of the price level and depreciating currency until the lower real interest rate target is relinquished, at which time the employment level will sink back to its equilibrium level. The presence of a high degree of indexation or full indexation means that this process unfolds very quickly, leaving a legacy of a higher price level and memories of only a brief rise of employment.

We cannot be sure that our discussion here has applied the right model or at any rate a good model to present-day Europe. But the chances that the real Europe is tolerably well described by it for the purposes at hand does give ground for doubting that monetary stimulus would be effective in restoring employment in Europe.

There is, second, the matter of the costliness of the side-effects of monetary stimulus. Governments apparently find little appeal in measures to combat a large rise of unemployment that entail a large rise of the price level – that is, a large upward (and nondiminishing) displacement of the price level path. A majority of the population can be assumed to oppose such measures as long as the unemployment rate is short of some level near 50 percent. Their support could be obtained only if their losses could be compensated by transfer payments financed out of the gains of those gaining; but if the effectiveness of monetary stimulus is slight there would be too small a margin of gains over losses to manage a successful program of compensation. (If one were to view the high unemployment as Pareto-efficient, which we do not, no surplus would exist to be mobilized.)

It is easy to see that economists weighing their estimates of the effectiveness of monetary stimulus against its side costs are disinclined to argue for a recovery program designed to rely primarily or heavily on monetary stimulus. Indeed it is natural in this setting for an economist's thoughts to turn to fiscal policy. Fiscal stimulus appears more attractive than monetary stimulus with respect to its side-effect on the price level – though less attractive in its side-effects on national wealth accumulation and the size of the public sector.

What, then, of the effectiveness of fiscal stimulus? Keynes sought to persuade Britain in the early years of the Depression that its problem was that investment lagged behind saving. This was a valid description of the problem if by (national) investment he meant the sum of domestic expenditure on capital goods (I) and net foreign investment, which is the balance of exports over imports ($X-M$). It was desired to have increased C in view of the level of $I + X - M$ or increased $I + X - M$ in view of the level of C. The problem was – and is now – how to accomplish either or both of these outcomes.

Keynes implied that a decreased supply of national saving would be a solution (although most of the contemporary discussion was about public works). Let us restrict ourselves here to increased consumer demand fed by a cut of personal income taxation or increased public expenditure on consumer goods –

[128]

hospital care, free school lunches, food and drug protection, and the rest. Alas, we are forced to observe that our models give a mixed reception to the thought that recovery in Europe might be floated on such a fiscal stimulus.

The customer-market model asserts that increased consumption-good spending by the home country serves to appreciate the currency, an effect which, taken alone, operates to reduce desired mark-ups and thus to expand employment. There is an additional expansionary effect that could be included, as the rise of the domestic real interest rate resulting from the expected reversal of the real exchange rate decreases the quantity of money demanded.[4] The other side of the coin, however, is that the same rise of the domestic real interest rate raises the desired mark-ups of firms (assuming that their owners do not buy their consumer goods solely from abroad), and this effect operates to contract employment. Finally, an increase of spending on consumer goods that is large in relation to world production, which a really large increase of European spending surely would be, would increase the foreign, or world, real interest rate, and that effect would operate to increase mark-ups too. The customer market model, therefore, does not seem to offer a ringing endorsement of increased consumer-good spending as an instrument of recovery.

The real-price-of-investment goods model is also somewhat ambiguous about increased consumer-good spending. With less than full indexation, which is the realistic assumption, it appears, there is an expansionary "Keynesian" effect on employment and the

[129]

product wage in the consumer good sector, in so far as the increased demand is large in relation to world output. But the stronger the degree of indexation the stronger is the crowding-out effect, via the higher real interest rate that results, upon employment in the investment-goods producing sector. Under full indexation, it appears, increased consumer demand in the home country has only an indirect effect on home-country employment, and this is a perverse effect through the channel of the world real rate of interest. The consumer price level and general wage level rise as output and employment in the investment-good sector fall. Thus, the two-sector model gives little encouragement to this sort of fiscal stimulus.

Finally, we note that the effects of fiscal stimulus directed at consumption upon employment via the capital-stock channel are also not favorable. If such stimulus would tend to slow the accumulation of capital in Europe, as our models (as currently structured) imply, it would tend to impede recovery rather than promote it, so far as this channel is concerned.

This brings us finally to fiscal stimulus in the form of increased spending on investment goods, either through government subsidies to private investment or government purchases of investment goods. This is the route to recovery that seems most likely – or least unlikely – to work. It would attack directly the unemployment present in the investment-goods sector in the case without wholesale tradability. If it raises the domestic real rate of interest it will to that extent have adverse effects on mark-ups; but the exchange-rate effects may be expected to have beneficial effects on mark-ups.

If in fact increased government spending in Europe in the 1930s had a good deal to do with the recovery of employment from the Depression, that success may be owed to the fact that most of that increased spending was for public works. It was capital expenditure. On purely empirical grounds alone, then, one feels inclined to believe that increased spending by the government on capital goods, through investment subsidies or direct spending, would work once more. If he were here, Lloyd George could do it now. And so can Europe.

Notes

1 Lloyd George, Address to Liberal candidates, March 1, 1929.
2 J. M. Keynes, "Can Lloyd George do it?", in Collected Writings of J. M. Keynes, vol. XIX: *Activities 1922–1929; The Return to Gold and Industrial Policy*, chapter 9, Macmillan/Cambridge University Press, 1981.
3 M. Wagner, "New variants of Keynesianism: could Lloyd George do it today?", Lecture, European University Institute, Florence, April 1986.
4 These two points were the focus of the small-country model in E. S. Phelps, "The significance of customer markets for the effects of budgetary policy in open economies," *Annales d'Economie et de Statistique*, no. 3, 1986. Reprint Series no. 330, Institute for International Economic Studies, University of Stockholm.

Selected References

Anyadike-Danes, M. and Fitoussi, J.-P., 1984: "Dimensions du problème de l'emploi en Europe et aux Etats-Unis", *Lettre de l'OFCE* no. 12, February.

Artus, P., Laroque, G. and Michel, G., 1984: "Estimation of a quarterly macro-economic model with quantity rationing," *Econometrica*, vol. 52, November.

Blanchard, O. J. and Summers, L. H., 1984: "Perspectives on high world real interest rates," *Brookings Papers on Economic Activity*, 1984:2 (Washington, DC: Brookings Institution).

Blanchard, O. J. and Summers, L. H., 1986: "Hysteresis and the European unemployment problem," Harvard Institute of Economic Research, Discussion Paper 1240, May (mimeo).

Bruno, M., 1986: "Aggregate supply and demand factors in OECD unemployment: an update," *Economica*, 53 (supplement).

Bruno, M. and Sachs, J. D., 1985: *Economics of Worldwide Stagflation*. Harvard University Press.

Daniel B., 1981: "The international transmission of economic disturbances under flexible exchange rates," *International Economic Review*, vol. 22, October.

Dehez, P. and Fitoussi, J.-P., 1986: "Wage indexation and macroeconomic fluctuations," in Wilfred Beckerman (ed.), *Wage Rigidity and Unemployment*. Baltimore: Johns Hopkins Press.

Dehez, P. and Fitoussi, J.-P., 1981: "Equilibres de stagflation et

[133]

indexation des salaires," in J.-P. Fitoussi and P.-A. Muet (eds) *Macrodynamique et déséquilibres*, Economica.

Dreze, J.-H., 1981: "Underemployment equilibria," *European Economic Review*, vol. 13, nos 1/2, February/March.

Dornbusch, R., 1980: *Open-Economy Macroeconomics*. New York: Basic Books.

Dornbusch, R., 1985: "Policy and performance links between LDC debtors and industrial nations," *Brookings Papers on Economic Activity*, 1985:2.

Feldstein, M., 1986: "US budget deficits and the European economies: resolving the political economy puzzle," *American Economic Review*, May.

Fitoussi, J.-P., 1983: "Modern macroeconomic theory: an overview," in J.-P. Fitoussi (ed.), *Modern Macroeconomic Theory*, Oxford: Basil Blackwell.

Fitoussi, J.-P. and others, 1985: *Real Wages and Unemployment, Report to the European Economic Community*. Brussels, December.

Fitoussi, J.-P., Le Cacheux, J., Lecointe, F. and Vasseur, C., 1986: "Taux d'intérêt réels et activité économique," *Observations et diagnostics économiques* no. 15, April.

Frenkel, J. and Razin, A., 1986: "Budget deficits and rates of interest in the world economy," *Journal of Political Economy*, June.

George, L., 1929: Address to Liberal candidates, March 1.

Gubian, A., Guillaumat-Tailliet, F. and Le Cacheux, J., 1986: "Fiscalité des entreprises et décision d'investissement," *Observations et diagnostics economiques*, no. 16, July.

Hall, R. E., 1970: "Unionism and the inflationary bias of labor markets," Berkeley, Calif. (mimeo).

Hall, R. E., 1986: "The relation between price and marginal cost in U.S. industry," NBER Working Paper no. 1785, January.

Hayashi, F., 1982: "Tobin's marginal q and average q: a neoclassical interpretation," *Econometrica*, 50, January.

Keynes, J. M., 1981: "Can Lloyd George do it?", in Collected Writings of J. M. Keynes, vol. XIX: *Activities 1922–1929: The Return to Gold and Industrial Policy*, chapter 9, Macmillan/ Cambridge University Press.

Krugman, P., 1984: "International aspects of U.S. monetary and fiscal policy," *Economics of Large Government Deficits*, Federal Reserve Bank of Boston.

Kurz, M., 1982: "Unemployment equilibrium in an economy with linked prices," *Journal of Economic Theory*, February.

Lindbeck, A. and Snower, D. J., 1986: "Wage setting, unemployment, and insider–outsider relations," *American Economic Review*, vol. 76, May.

Malinvaud, E., 1977: *The Theory of Unemployment Reconsidered*. Oxford: Basil Blackwell.

Malinvaud, E., 1987: "The legacy of European stagflation," *European Economic Review*, vol. 31, nos 1/2, February/March.

Mundell, R. A., "Capital mobility and stabilization policy under fixed and flexible exchange rates," *Canadian Journal of Economics and Political Science*, November.

Mundell, R. A., 1964: "A reply: capital mobility and size," *Canadian Journal of Economics and Political Science*, vol. 30, August.

Okun, A., 1982: *Prices and Quantities*, Washington D.C.: Brookings Institute.

Phelps, E. S., 1972: *Inflation Policy and Unemployment Theory* London: Mcmillan.

Phelps, E. S., 1978: "Commodity-supply shock and full-employment monetary policy," *Journal of Money, Credit and Banking*, vol. 10, May.

Phelps, E. S., 1986: "The effectiveness of macropolicies in small open-economy dynamic aggregate models," Temi di Discussione no. 63, Banca d'Italia, May.

Phelps, E. S., 1986: "The significance of customer markets for the effects of budgetary policy in open economies," *Annales d'Economie et de Statistique*, no. 3, 1986, reprint series no. 330. Stockholm: Institute for International Economic Studies, University of Stockholm.

Phelps, E. S. and Winter, S. G., Jr, 1970: "Optimal price policy under atomistic competition," in E. S. Phelps and others, *Microeconomic Foundation of Employment and Inflation Theory*, New York: Norton.

Sachs, J. D., 1986: "High unemployment in Europe," Working

[135]

Paper no. 1830, National Bureau of Economic Research, February.

Salop, S. C., 1979: "A model of the natural rate of unemployment," *American Economic Review*, vol. 69, no. 1, March.

Sneessens, H. and Dreze, J.-H., 1986: "A discussion of Belgian unemployment, combining traditional concepts and disequilibrium econometrics," *Economica*, 53, S89–S119.

Wagner, M., 1986: "New variants of Keynesianism: could Lloyd George do it today?", Lecture, European University Institute, Florence, April.

Index

Pages numbered in **bold** include tables, in *italics* include figures.
Page numbers followed by 'n' refer to notes.

aggregative customer-market
    model, *see*
    customer-market model
aggregative orthodox model,
    see orthodox model
appreciation
    expected rate of future
    real 64
    of dollar 8, 27
Artus, P. 11n
augmented orthodox model,
    see orthodox model
austerity, fiscal, *see* fiscal
    austerity

Beckerman, W. 11n, 96n
Blanchard, Olivier 100, 123n,
    124n
Bruno, Michael 11n, 39–40,
    51n

budget surplus, structural, *see*
    structural budget surplus

capital
    allocation of 68
    expenditure, public sector 2
    formation, investment in
    gross fixed 28, **30**
    goods, *see* capital goods
    perfect mobility 36
    shock transmission
    and 66–78
    stock of, *see* capital stock
    use and maintenance
    of 74–5
    user cost of 19–21
    evolution of 19, *20–1*
    see also investment
capital goods
    investment in 28, *31*

real price **32**
relative price   32–3
capital stock   115
  contraction of
    European   67–8
  decline and
    employment   90–1
  effects on
    employment   67–9, *70*,
    71–5
  hysteresis
    mechanism   119–20
  recovery and   130
  slow down in   93–4
cash balances, real   39
cash flow   76–7
competitiveness
  gain of   27
  increased by
    depreciation   54
consumer demand   79–80
consumer goods, price
  level   55, 129–30
consumer price index   39, 54
contradictory movement   89,
  103–4
contracts
  Edgeworth-optimal   73–4
  indexation in   79
Coolidge, Calvin   94n
corporate taxation, direct   19,
  20
credit, interest rate
  effects   76–7
crowded in   9
crowding out   2, 9, 98, 130
  of investment   111

currencies, *see* depreciation;
  exchange rates *and*
  individual currencies
customer-market
  model   58–60, 111
  aggregative   58–60, *61*, 62–5
  recovery and   129
  wage share depression
    and   64
customer markets   56–64

Daniel, B.   51n
deficits, budgetary   100, 101
Dehez, P.   11n, 12n, 96n
demand
  consumer   79–80
  shocks   78–89
demand side
  explanations
    fiscal austerity
      hypothesis   97–112
    hysteresis effect   117–23
    tight money
      hypothesis   112–17
  modelling   58
Denmark   104
depreciation   102–3, 127
  allowances   19
  expected rate of future
    real   64–5
  increased competitiveness
    from   54
destimulus, *see* fiscal austerity
  at home; fiscal remedies
direct corporate taxation   19,
  20

dollar
· appreciation, consequences
   of 27
  counterbalancing real
   appreciation of 8
  exchange rate
   movements 14, **15**, 16–17
Dornbusch, Rudiger 38, 50n,
  51n
Dreze, J.-H. 11n

Edgeworth-optimal
  contracts 73–4
employability 118–19
employment 33–4
  accelerated retirment 54–5
  capital-stock effects
   on 67–9, *70*, 71–5
  in home country 72–3
  fiscal austerity and 102–3
  insider–outsider
   theory 120–2
  micro–macro models 90
  neoclassical 90
  net job creations **33**
  New Classical
   macroeconomics 90
  subsidies and 69–72
  supply-price effects 106,
  108
  tight money and 113–15
  see also labor; unemployment
essential aggregative orthodox
  model, *see* orthodox model
European Monetary System 8
exchange rates 14, **15**, 16–17
  fixed 36

fluctuating under monetarist
  policy 36, 37
  see also appreciation;
  currencies; depreciation
expansionary movement 88,
  129
expectations 48
  inflation rates 49–50
  reduced, of real interest
   rates 101
expenditure
  real national 45
  world investment 55
  see also investment

Federal Republic of Germany,
  see Germany (FRG)
Feldstein, M. 12n
filling in 98
financing, *see* credit
fiscal austerity at home 2, 4,
  97–112
  demand effect of *107*, 108
fiscal depreciation
  allowances 19
fiscal remedies 125, 128–31
  capital stock channel 130
  increased spending on
   investment goods 130
fiscal stimulus abroad 37, 38,
  39, 46, 47, 48, 53
  in aggregative
   customer-market
   model 60, *61*
  destimulus at home and 102
  investment-goods-prices
   model 85–6, 88

Fitoussi, J.-P.   11n, 12n, 95n, 96n
Frenkel, J.   123n

general equilibrium model   4
  with rationing   4
  see also two-country models
George, David Lloyd, see
  Lloyd George, David
Germany (FRG)
  fiscal austerity in   98, 102, 103–4
  nominal interest rates   104
  restrictive monetary
    policy   8
  structural budget
    surplus   **109**, 110
goods, intermediate   38, 40
gross domestic product
  growth rate of deflator   *115*
  growth rates of   **3**
Gubian, A.   34n
Guillaumat-Tailliet, F.   34n

Hall, R. E.   94n, 123n
Hayashi, F.   95n
Hicks   45
hysteresis effect   117–23
  capital stock
    mechanism   119–20
  employability
    mechanism   118–19
  insider–outsider employment
    theory   120–2

indexation   79–80, 81–4, 86, 93, 116, 121

in contracts   79
indexed wages   54, 73–4
recovery and   126, 127, 130
  see also wages
inflation   127
  imported   8
  rate
    expected   49–50
    non-accelerating, of
      unemployment   6
interdependence, national   36, 37
interest rates   2
  domestic austerity following
    stimulus abroad   *107*, 108
  high in US   62
  labor hoarding and   75–6
  long-term   17, **18**, 34n
  mark-ups and   63–4
  nominal   102, 103, 104, **105**, 106
    increasing   117
  orthodox transmission
    theory and   57
  real   17–19, 26
    cash flow and   76–7
    domestic   103
    employment and   75–6
    foreign shock drives
      up   88
    hoards of labor and   54
    price setting functions
      and   63
    target of monetarist
      policy   126–7
    use and maintenance of
      capital and   74–5

wage share depression
and 64
intermediate goods 34, 40
investment
behind saving 128–9
in capital goods 28, *31*, 32
capital stock and 119–20
crowding out of 111
decline in 66–7
diminishing-return
effect 42
domestic 42–3
expenditure
home 61–2
reduced 62
world 55
gross fixed capital
formation 28, **30**
marginal efficiency after
tax 101
subsidies 19, 53, 69–72,
101, 130
beneficial demand effect
of 56
instituted abroad 46,
47–8
world 55, 95n
see also capital; expenditure;
fiscal stimulus abroad
investment-goods
prices 78–89
model 80–9, *82, 87*
recovery and 129–30
with non-tradability 86,
87, 88–9
with tradability *82*, 83–6
reduction of 117

Italy 4
structural budget
surplus **109**, 110

Japan 100

Keynes, John Maynard 5,
125, 128, 131n
Keynesian hypothesis 2,
97–112
Krugman, P. 94n
Kurz, M. 12n

labor
adjustment-cost
hypothesis 75
capital stock decline
and 90–1
hoards of 75–6
disinvesting in 54
markets, immobility 4
productivity, *see* labor
productivity
reallocation of 90
see also employment
labor productivity 22, 27–8
average *29*
capital stock decline
and 72–3
marginal 5
Laroque, G. 11n
Le Cacheux, J. 34n, 95n
Lecointe, F. 95n
Lindbeck, A. 123n
Lloyd George, David 125,
131n

maintenance of capital 74–5

Malinvaud, E. 11n
marginal productivity 5
  real marginal-revenue 91–2
mark (currency) 8
mark-ups 16–17, 23, *24–6*, 27, 34n
  European driven up 62
  European firms, in customer markets 54
  firm's policy and prices 57
  interest rates and 63–4
  US reduced 62
Michel, G. 11n
models
  customer-market 58–60, *61*, 62–5, 111, 129
  general equilibrium 4, 7
  investment-goods price 80–9, 129–30
  Mundell–Fleming 36, 98
  orthodox 40–3, *44*, 45–50
    aggregative, capital-stock effects on 67–9, *70*, 71–5
    augmented, capital stock shocks in *70*
  Tobin–Sargent type 48
  two-country 7, 36
  two-sector 111, 130
  see also orthodox theory
monetarism 57
  fluctuating exchange rate 36, 37
  liberal 56, 57
  restrictive policy 8
monetarist hypothesis 112–17, 114–15

timing of unemployment rise 115–16
  see also tight money abroad
monetarist remedies 125–8
  cost of side-effects 127–8
  domestic real interest rate and 126–7
money
  demand for 73, 102
  supply, see money supply
  velocity of 2, 38, 45
  see also cash flow; tight money abroad
money supply 58
  growth rates 113, *114*
  repeated suppression of growth rate 116
  timing of unemployment rises and 115–16
  see also tight money hypothesis
Muet, P.-A. 12n
Mundell, Robert A. 36, 50n
Mundell–Fleming model 36, 98

non-accelerating inflation rate of unemployment (NAIRU) 6

oil-price shocks
  1979 6, 7
  differences in periods following 13
Okun, Arthur 95n
orthodox model 40–3, *44*, 45–50

aggregative   40–3, *44*,
45–50
    capital-stock effects
        on   67–9, *70*, 71–5
    augmented, capital shocks
        in   *70*
orthodox theory   35–51
    qualifications   38–9
    standard propositions   36–8
    see also orthodox model
output   *107*, 108

Phelps, E. S.   94n, 95n, 123n,
124n, 131n
Pigou   4
price index, consumer
    goods   39, 54
price linkages   4
prices
    consumer good price
        level   55, 129–30
    future   102
    industry   57
    investment-good   78–89
    market-clearing level   66
    rise in   127–8
    setting functions, interest
        rates and   63
    supply   57
product wage   55
productivity, *see* labor;
    marginal productivity
profitability   21–2
public expenditure   2, 9, 98
    see also fiscal austerity at
    home

rate of interest, *see* interest
    rates
Razin, A.   123n
Reagan tax cut   53
real cash balances   39
real interest rates, *see* interest
    rates, real
real investment-goods-price
    model, *see* investment-good
    prices, model
real wages   22
    gap   5–6
    high employment wage
        compared   5
    rigidity   4, 5, 120
    stickiness   73, 91–2
recovery, *see* remedies
recruitment   75–6
remedies
    fiscal   125, 128–31
    monetarist   125–8
Ricardo, David   36, 40
Robertson, D. H.   75

Sachs, Jeffrey D.   11n, 39–40
Salop, S. C.   95n
savings   128–9
shock transmission
    capital mechanism in   66–78
    customer markets
        and   56–64
    economy response   59–60,
        61
    investment-good prices
        in   78–89
slump
    magnitude of   1–2

persistence of 89–94
recovery from 125–31
supply-price view 89–94
Sneessens, H. 11n
Snower, D. J. 123n
stagflation 7
Stock market prices 64, 101
structural budget surplus **99**,
100
inflation-adjusted **109**, 110
unemployment rate
and 110
subsidies, *see* investment,
subsidies
Summers, Lawrence H. 100,
123n, 124n
supply curves, competitive 43
supply-side effects 5–6, 39, 40
capital stock transmission
of 67–75
of investment subsidies 56
price effects 106, 108
surpluses, structural budget,
see structural budget
surplus

taxation
direct corporate 19, *20*
Reagan tax cut 53
see also fiscal austerity at
home; fiscal remedies;
fiscal stimulus abroad
tight money abroad 37–8, 45,
47, 48, 56
in aggregative
customer-market

model 60, *61*
investment-goods-prices
model 84–5, 88
tight money
hypothesis 112–17
Tobin–Sargent type
models 48
trade
intermediate goods 38, 40
two-way 40
training costs 75–6
Treasury view 1920s 100–1
two-country models 7, 36
two-sector models 111
recovery and 130

unemployment
classical nature of 6–7
differences in rises 110–11
equilibrium rate 92
natural 92
non-accelerating inflation
rate of 6
rate 3
natural 119
structural budget surplus
and 110
world 122
social costs 119
timing of rise 115–16
see also employment; labor
unionization 4, 121
United Kingdom
fiscal austerity in 98, 102
see also fiscal austerity at
home

nominal interest rates   104
user cost of capital, *see* capital,
   user cost of

Vasseur, C.   95n
velocity of money   2, 38, 45

wages
   contractual   54, 73–4
   Edgeworth-optimal
      contracts   73–4

high employment   5
indexation, *see* indexation
insider–outsider employment
   theory and   120–2
product   55
real, *see* real wages
share of   21–3
   depressed   64
   rate of change of   **22**
Wagner, Michael   125, 131n
Winter, S. G.   94n
world investments   55, 95n